Your First Bestseller

How to Self-Publish a Successful Book on Amazon

by Mike Fishbein

www.mfishbein.com

Table of Contents

Introduction

To date, I've self-published over 15 books, launching several into Amazon's bestseller list and learning a lot along the way. I've made rookie errors and failed dismally, at times doubting myself and my new chosen career path. But no matter how spectacularly I have fallen, I've always brushed myself off, got back up and put my lessons into practice.

A lot of the books I've written have been failures. In the beginning I'd quickly scrap a book together about something I thought was interesting, hire a cheap designer to fling some words and colors together, and publish it on Amazon hoping people would find it, as if by magic.

Did they find it? No.

Did I sell books? Needless to say… no.

But I'm not the only one who has made these mistakes. Most books fail.

Fortunately, through trial and error, I've now learned the best practices for self-publishing a successful book on Amazon. From writing a book that people want buy, to building an e-mail list to garner lifelong customers, to hiring the best editors, designers and formatters for the job, as well as knowing where and how to promote my book once published.

Simply following the steps I outline in this book has helped me to launch multiple books into Amazon's bestseller list. Now, I make thousands of dollars in passive income each month doing what I love: writing.

If you're waiting for that perfect moment to self-publish a book, it's never going to arrive. There is no best time to start anything. Your mind will be filled with doubts and excuses until there's no more time to count. My advice? Start now. Just take the leap. This is what I did, and believe me, it is paying off big time.

You've got your hands on this book, so that's a good first step! You've already come further along your path than most would-be authors. You've made the decision to self-publish your own book and now you want to know the best way of doing it, as well as how to turn it into a bestseller. After reading this, the process of self-publishing a successful book on Amazon will seem a whole lot less daunting, even easy!

Looking back over my experiences, self-publishing a successful book on Amazon is not actually that complicated. You just have to nail a few fundamental steps. This book covers those fundamentals.

A Little About Me, The Author

I am a self-published author and inbound marketer. I've written multiple books on personal development and marketing. I've worked with startups and fortune 500 companies on content marketing and product management. I've had my writing featured on top sites like *Entrepreneur*, *Huffington Post* and *The Next Web*. Previously I worked at a tech startup in New York doing marketing and product management.

Feel free to check out my blog at mfishbein.com and my books at mfishbein.com/amazon.

Additional Resources

In this book, I share with you all of the basics of self-publishing a successful book on Amazon. However, if you really want to succeed as a self-published author and make it onto the bestseller list, there is so much more you can learn in order to succeed.

I really want you to succeed. So, I'm going to give you my Ultimate Amazon Self-Publishing Checklist for free. In this comprehensive checklist I'll walk you through each and every step you need to take to self-publish a successful book. From coming up with a book idea right through to the best marketing practices post launch, it's all in there for you.

The Ultimate Amazon Self-Publishing Checklist

I know how daunting the task of self-publishing your own book can be, especially if you are new to the business. Not only do you need to come up with an awesome idea and unique selling point, but then there's the overwhelming process of writing, publishing and marketing to tackle too. After over a dozen book launches, I've learned a few things about how to self-publish a book.

To make the process as smooth and successful as possible for you, I've created this comprehensive 29 step checklist to self-publishing on Amazon that you can print out and reference every step of the way .

>> Get the checklist for free here. <<
(http://mfishbein.com/selfpub-checklist-book)

Chapter 1

How To Become a Writing Machine

You don't need to be a world-class writer to self-publish your own book. I was a horrible writer when I first started. I'm still not the best writer. I'm probably about average at best. But, my writing has gotten better and can only continue improving by incorporating a few simple practices into my routine.

The best way to learn how to write is to read and write yourself. Find someone you can model. For me, I like to model my writing styles off of James Altucher and Neil Patel. James writes extremely personal stories and publishes blog posts almost everyday. He's also not afraid of being controversial.

Neil posts highly detailed educational posts.
I highly suggest finding some writers to base your style off of. Read their stuff, get used to their voice and style, then, start writing. It's okay if you're not good right now. Like I mentioned before, learn by doing. You will get better.

After that, it just comes down to writing more...

The Truth About Finding Time To Write

It's not always easy to make time to write.

For me, this is how I get it done.

I wake up at 6am. I do some light stretching and breathing. I write down 10 ideas (http://mfishbein.com/10-ideas-james-altucher/). Then I write.

Making self-publishing books a priority means I had to trim a lot of the fat from my life. I had to get rid of what I can live without, in order to pursue what I want.

I go to sleep at 10pm. Why so early? I do this so I can I wake up at 6AM and be writing before 7AM.

There's nothing else for me to be doing at this time.

Nothing on my calendar. No meetings or parties.

"How do you find time to write? How do you find time to do anything in your life?"

You prioritize it.

You sit down. You fire down some coffee. You put your headphones on. Listen to The Disco Biscuits (or the music of your choice). And you do the work.

Do you have trouble finding the time to go to work?

Stop watching TV. Stop drinking. Tell your friends to get out.

If you're not willing to cut out even a few extras from your life, you won't be able make writing and self-publishing your book the priority it needs to be.

So... do the work!

Forming the Habit

Writing is a core competency of any successful self-publisher. I sell my writing as ebooks. I then write blog posts to market the ebooks.

I formed the habit of writing by forcing myself to hit publish (https://medium.com/@mfishbein/hitting-the-publish-button-everyday-f780aa59936c) everyday when I first got started. Even now when I go through slumps, even if I'm not proud of the writing, I hit publish. Don't know what to write in the conclusion? I hit publish anyway.

Writing simply requires opening your laptop and moving your fingers. I've done it a million times before for everything from sending emails to searching on Google.

The physical acts of so many healthy, productive habits are so, so easy, but we build them up into these monumental hurdles in our head. Writing is one of those.

Accountability

I had been trying to start and maintain a writing habit for about two years. The tyranny all ultimately came to an end when I tried this one simple strategy. A strategy that I had heard about a dozen times before but didn't bother to try...

I got an accountability partner to call me everyday just to make sure I publish something. Accountability works because it adds social pressure to otherwise self-directed work. This can be especially valuable if you're a solopreneur who doesn't have partners or a boss to report to everyday.

Accountability partners help each other implement and maintain their commitments and desired habits by tracking each other's progress.

When I sit on my couch deciding whether to write, thinking about the irrational fear over putting my butt in the chair, opening my laptop, and moving my fingers, I think about having to tell my accountability partner that I failed. It's a lot easier to let yourself down than it is to let someone else down.

To find an accountability partner, you could try asking friends who are into personal development, or posting in relevant Facebook groups. I met my partner through an entrepreneurship group we're both members of.

We try to call each other everyday, since we're both working on daily habits. Just for a quick five minute check in. If we're not able to connect by phone, we just share our output via Facebook messenger. I definitely recommend daily check ins, and via phone if you can.

Accountability partners can be extremely helpful, and I'm probably not the first person to tell you that. So give it a try and see if it helps you make those habits stick like it has for me. It can especially be useful when you're starting a big venture like self-publishing a book, so I highly suggest it.

Getting Over Writer's Block

Have you ever watched a movie where the villain says something like "You can run, but you can't hide" and wonder what the hell that means?
Well, it applies to writer's block, because you can't hide from it. You can't really run from it either, the best thing you can do it learn how to overcome it. Experiencing writer's block used to drive me crazy.

As a self-published author (http://mfishbein.com/amazon) writing is my lifeblood. I always have several blog posts and books in draft, and more ideas in the pipeline. However, often times my biggest trouble is simply putting my butt in the chair, my fingers on the keys, and replacing the blank page (http://blog.write-track.co.uk/writers/how-to-get-past-that-blank-page-and-write-your-first-book/) and blinking cursor with my thoughts.

Since late 2014, I've been somewhat of a content creating machine. I was cranking out a book about once every month and half. I even wrote a book about How to Write a Book in 10 Days (http://selfpubtoday.com/writing) that I wrote in just (you guessed it!) 10 days. But, I wasn't always like this.

To overcome procrastination and get in the rhythm of writing, I forced myself to write something, anything, everyday. Set yourself a schedule and just do it.

I started doing this the day I decided to take my self-publishing seriously, and it'll continue to be that way until my fingers can't move anymore. Everyday, I'll write about whatever my mind is most fixated on. It could be an interesting conversation I had, something I've learned recently, a strategy or tactic I've been using, or an opinion I have about a current event.

Whenever I go a few days without writing, it gets harder and harder to do. It reminds me that I need to go back to writing everyday. Writing is like a muscle, if you don't exercise it, it will atrophy.

Starting a book from scratch is like starting a new exercise regimen: you need to build up the muscle, ability, flexibility, etc. in order to get yourself in writing shape. From there, the main focus goes to maintaining your results.

After I got in the habit of writing something every day, I started writing longer and more valuable blog posts that I could use later in my books. I no longer needed to force myself to write everyday because I could trust myself to publish a valuable post once per week.

Whenever I feel writer's block creeping up on me, I always go back to basics and force myself to hit the publish button.

Key Takeaways

Sure, there are tons of people talking about the best strategies to self-publish a book, but that's not all you need to hit the bestseller list. The hardest part is simply getting started. If you can't get started and stick with it, then you'll never make money or achieve your goals.

When it comes to writing, your strategies will evolve and improve over time. It's okay if you're not a strong writer early on. The best way to get better is by practicing. Also, building a habit of writing is just as important. You're never going to find the time for writing, you need to make time for it.

If you're still stuck, I have two more solutions for you. If you've got the money and know what good writing looks like, you can hire freelancers (http://mfishbein.com/hire-freelance-writers/) to write for you. Or, you can use transcription (https://medium.com/@mfishbein/how-to-triple-your-writing-using-transcription-2e1b6b74068) as a way to write more if you don't have a lot of time to sit down and type.

Chapter 2

How To Write a Book That People Want To Read

You're not the only self-publishing author, believe me, there is a lot of competition out there. No matter what your chosen topic or niche, chances are there are a lot of other authors trying to sell similar content.

When I first started writing I was creating what I thought was valuable content (http://mfishbein.com/awesome-content/), but my Google Analytics told me otherwise. It was only when I learned the tactics to writing awesome content that I list below, did I start seeing traffic to my site which lead to a bigger audience for my books.

To be a successful self-published author, you need to write better content than the rest. Here's how you can do that.

Provide Value

What's important when it comes to a great books is providing value to your readers. Hook them in by creating an entertaining story, but make sure they get something useful out of it too. Don't just entertain; educate. If you don't provide real value, readers may feel they are getting a raw deal.

How do you provide value? My ebook, How to Create Awesome Content (http://www.amazon.com/How-Create-Awesome-Content-Marketing-ebook/dp/B00ZYGH27O/ref=asap_bc?ie=UTF8) mentions everything you need to know about providing value. Below are a few examples:

Listen for Questions

It's important to pay attention to what your audience wants to learn. Be sure to read your emails from readers and be aware of and pay attention to what people are asking of you.

For example, I get a lot of emails from people asking where they should be guest blogging and how to do it. After getting the same question multiple times, I wrote an entire blog post on it (http://mfishbein.com/entrepreneurs-guide-guest-blogging/). Then, I kept getting more questions, so I wrote an entire ebook (http://www.amazon.com/Guest-Blogging-Master-Class-Subscribers-ebook/dp/B00XF51KWY) about it!

Do you have answers for the questions your readers are asking? If so, is there a way you can deliver these answers through your book? Paying attention to this, as it is a great way to assess demand and to know which content to deliver.

Use the Keyword Planner

When thinking about what to write, look at your keyword research. Take advantage of Google's Keyword Planner. Doing this allows you to mold the content you're going to write, to what your intended audience is searching for. If they are searching for it on Google, it is a clear indication of demand.

Do What's Already Working

Just because someone else has written about it, doesn't mean you can't put your own spin on it, or do it better. Of course, you'll have to find a creative way to make your book different from the others out there (never ever plagiarize), but it can definitely be done.

There are sites you can use to check out what sort of content is being shared and how posts are ranking. Buzzsumo (http://buzzsumo.com/) is a great tool for this and offers a trial plan if you're curious to see how it all works. Not only can you use Buzzsumo to search for related sites with similar content, but you can use their analytics to measure how your content is ranking compared to a competitor.

Get Obsessed with Helping Your Audience

Providing value is essential to any business. If you're not providing value, then why would anyone pay you money?

Use customer development tactics (http://mfishbein.com/customer-development-questions-create-content/) to figure out what your audience's problems are. Validate demand for your ideas and get feedback on your content.

Go big. Be more specific, more transparent, more comprehensive and more authentic.

Tell stories. Humans are naturally drawn to stories. Don't be afraid to share your personal experience and provide some takeaways from real life experiences.

Providing value to people is crucial to success in any business – passive income, software, service, or otherwise. The best way to provide value is to understand what your audience is looking for, and then become obsessed with helping them find it.

I learned this the hard way, after spending hours and hours on a video course on a topic that people had little demand for.

Bleed on the First Line

Now more than ever, we, as consumers, have short attention spans. Mobile technology and increasingly efficient computers have made us driven to find the next article, video, or item to give that would give us gratification. What people choose to read largely depends on having an enticing headline (hence the rise of the clickbait titles) and an even better introduction that inspires the reader to keep reading. The important truth is that, in order to get any attention online, we need to tell them why they should give us any time. And do this immediately, lest they divert their attention to someone else.

How is this done? I've noticed that many writers tend to make their first line a shocker.
For example, in James Altucher's "Ten Lessons I Learned from Shark Tank,"
(http://www.jamesaltucher.com/2012/02/ten-lessons-i-learned-from-shark-tank/) his first line reads, "I just gave up all parenting responsibilities this weekend to

Mark Cuban. Meaning, my kids and I watched eight straight episodes of Shark Tank."

I don't know about you, but this caught my attention. How many fathers would openly admit to throwing aside responsibility?

Furthermore, how many kids could be convinced to watch the same adult television show for 8 straight hours? I had to find out, which is to say, I kept reading.

How did I capture your attention at the beginning of this book? I told you a little bit of my own story to let you know that I've been where you are. Hopefully me baring all to you was enough to get you hooked enough to read on.

When writing your book description for Amazon, it is especially important to draw potential readers in with the first line. Write something catchy, surprising or thought provoking that will tempt them to keep reading, and of course, buy the book to get the full story. Then, write a great introduction that gets them excited to read the rest of the book.

Test Your Topics First

Randomly, Louis C.K. will drop by at a small open mic in New York City to do a set for free so he can test his new jokes. Why? He wants to make sure they're funny (valuable). It's much safer for him to try his new material out on a crowd of 200 rather than a crowd of 20,000.

Before you get too stuck into your writing, test your topics out first. One way I test out book ideas is by writing a blog post about the topic first. If I think of an idea for a book or chapter, sometimes I'll just tweet the title or some of the main points before I even write it. I'm just looking to see if people will reply or retweet. If there is engagement with that tweet it's an indication that there's demand.

Writing takes time. Your time is valuable. So, it's smart to create "minimum viable content" before spending hours and hours creating the final product.

Minimum viable content on a book might be a blog post. So, write a blog post to see if that gets traction for that content or that topic. Minimum viable content for a blog post might be a tweet or a Facebook post in a private group. There are certainly many different ways you can start with something small then build on it. Keep your audience in mind and write so that you can attract more readers and customers no matter what.

Teaching a webinar or in-person class is another way to really get in front of your audience and get feedback before you start writing. This enables you to get qualitative feedback from your audience.

I've done this first hand. Actually, this is how I

developed my book, How to Build an Awesome Professional Network (http://mfishbein.com/network). It started out as an in-person class. Yet, I didn't even decide to do the in-person class until I had written a few blog posts that were getting good reactions from people.

Chapter 3

All the Small Things That Go a Long Way

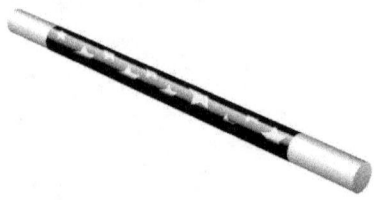

It's not enough to simply write an awesome book that readers will love. That alone won't set it flying off the shelves. To sell your book, and sell it well, you need to put it in front of your target customers and make it enticing enough that they'll have no choice but to buy it.

To do this, you'll need a catchy title, an eye-catching cover design that makes it stand out from all the rest, and a book description for Amazon clearly explaining the value readers will gain.

But, before all the fancy stuff, you need to ensure your book is formatted optimally for reading on Kindle devices.

Formatting

When it comes to formatting my books, the method I've found to work really well is quite simple. I draft up the content for my books using Google Docs; this includes copy, links and images. The benefits of using Google Docs is that it's easy to collaborate with other contributors (such as writers, editors, and readers who can give you feedback before publishing), your work is automatically saved as you go along, and all your docs, images, keyword research and any other content file you may need, is all stored in one place.

When I am ready for formatting, I source a professional book formatter through Upwork (https://www.upwork.com/). I have her convert my book into one of KDP's required formats (https://kdp.amazon.com/help?topicId=A2GF0UFHIY G9VQ) and ensure that my book reads well on Kindle devices. You can handle this yourself if you prefer, I just find it easier to hire a professional. You will then need a different format for paperback via Createspace. That will be covered in Part 2 of this book.

Hiring writers, editors, designers and formatters

To produce a book that really stands out and lends you credibility as an author, you'll likely need professionals to help you be a cut above the rest. While I do the bulk of the planning, writing and marketing of my books myself, I also work with freelancers to give them a professional polish.

Hiring freelancers means you can divide and delegate tasks, freeing you up to concentrate on your areas of strength or preference. Having more hands on deck also enables you to create more content and faster, meaning more money in your pocket.

There are a lot of freelancers out there, but not all of them are capable of delivering top notch work. Finding the right freelancer for the job can be a challenge when you have to navigate notorious pitfalls like late deliverables, poor communication, or quantity-over-quality type content.

To ensure you get the quality you're looking for, you need to be very clear on what you want before you start searching. By taking the time to plan your strategy according to your needs, budget, goals, etc., you can save time and money in the long run.

Identify your needs and budget

The more you know what you want, the better directions you can give. The better directions you can give, the easier it is to find someone to complete the project. In general, you'll get what you pay for so decide beforehand what value to set the work at.

For example, if you're looking for a detailed illustrative cover, you made need to handle someone with both graphic design and free hand drawing skills.

If you want a really great cover, which I recommend, you'll have to pay at least $100. Good writers usually cost upwards of $0.10 per word and formatters range from about $25 to $50 per book.

Put up a job posting

Unless you already have a suitable freelancer on hand, once you know what you want, you now need to create a job posting that is as specific as possible to get the best results. When searching for writers, editors and designers, be sure to include a lot of detail such as style, purpose, quantity (for writers), deadline and budget. Include references and examples they can work off.

For formatters, simplify the process by having the final copy for your book laid out neatly in a Google Doc and include and be specific about any stylistic requirements you may have.

There are a bunch of reputable freelance sites on the web but I use mainly Upwork (https://www.upwork.com/) to source my formatters, CloudPeeps (https://www.cloudpeeps.com/) or referrals for my writers and again, referrals for my book cover designers.

Be Selective

You've got to filter out a lot of noise to find the suitable person for the job. One tip for weeding through applications is to include a specific instruction somewhere within your application.

For example, at the end of one of my job postings, I wrote, "Tell me about similar work you have done and how you would approach this job."

Most people won't do this, so you should only read the applications of people that followed your instructions. Anyone who can't follow these simple directions is probably not someone you want working for you.

Pricing

Once you've published your book, if you don't have a huge following or access to someone else's, it may be beneficial start off by offering it for free the first few days. Although this may seem counterintuitive at first, there are benefits to this in the long term. Offering your book for free will give you a boost in downloads and allows your friends a chance to read it and give a verified review. The downloads also indicate to Amazon that there is demand for the book, encouraging them to promote it further.

When potential customers browse Amazon and see that others have downloaded your book and taken the time to write reviews, the likelihood of them purchasing it for themselves increases. It also indicates to Amazon that they should be promoting it to more readers. I'll get into more detail about this later.

Once your free stint is up, increase the price marginally to $0.99 for about a week to keep getting those paid downloads. After that, I'd suggest upping it to between $2.99- $3.99 depending on length of the book. Selling your book at $2.99- $9.99 gives you a 70% royalty cut. Pricing it at anything above or below that only gives you 30% in royalty.

If you already have a large following, you may want to launch at $0.99 and then raise to $3.99 or more.

You need to ask yourself: is your book for generating leads or is it for making money? Choose your pricing based on your intended outcome.

Kindle Unlimited

July 1, 2015 marked the launch of Amazon's new policy for authors with books offered on Kindle Owner's Lending Library or Kindle Unlimited which could change the future of the publishing industry. As a self-published author on Amazon, you may want to read this (http://mfishbein.com/amazon-policy-selfpublished-authors/).

Here's a bit about what you need to know about KDP Select:

- This subscription system is optional and there are more platforms other than Amazon (though, note that Amazon has a larger reader-base).
- This only affects those whose books are borrowed, not sold, meaning that if a book is purchased then an author will still receive the same amount of money as they would have before July 1, 2015.
- This process hurts poorly written, shorter books. Thus it encourages higher quality content from authors.
- The new policy helps to improve Amazon's brand as it helps to filter the quality of the

books, influencing authors to write higher quality content.

- If by chance, some authors cannot improve the quality of their writing, they may choose to leave KDP, which allocates more funds to the smaller amount of remaining authors.

Book marketing

To give yourself the best chance of success, you need a clear marketing plan in place before the ink on your first page dries. Ask yourself, "who is my market and what value is my book providing them?" If your book needs to meet a specific need or solve a particular problem to sell. Building an e-mail list is a critical component in finding out exactly what your reader's wants and needs are and tailoring your book for this. We'll cover this in the next chapter.

Part 3 of this book is on marketing, but it is worth considering your marketing strategy while you are writing and before you publish.

Chapter 4

How to Design the Perfect Book Cover

No matter what people say, we do judge a book by its cover. It's the first point of contact before we've even flipped to the blurb on the back or opened to the first page.

With so many ebooks out there, you need a book cover that immediately illustrates what your book is about and differentiates it from all the rest. Books with good graphics as well as eye-catching colors and fonts attract more potential customers than those that blend into the background.

Your book's cover design is one element you don't want to skimp on. A lot of authors get this wrong, mistakenly believing they can just throw something together last minute or hire a cheap designer to do it for them. In the beginning, I made this mistake and it hurt my sales, it was a lesson I had to learn fast. No matter how awesome your content is, if you get the cover wrong, potential readers may not even bother to get in far enough to find that out.

Below are a couple of tips I have gained along the way on how to create a kick ass cover.

Tips for a cover design that sells

1. Have a clear concept

Think of your cover as an advertisement for your book. Would you buy a pack of beef with a picture of the abattoir on it? No, chances are you'd rather see a picture of a happy cow frolicking in a field. Packaging is meant to make us feel good and convince us to buy a product, luring us by the value within. In this case 100% top grade beef from a cow that's lived a long and happy life. Book covers work the same way.

Before you even begin, you need to have a very clear idea of what you want to convey with your cover. Think carefully about the tone and message of your book. What value does it hold for readers? Who is your ideal target audience? Put yourself in the shoes of your readers and design a cover that tailors to their tastes.

2. Be bold

Now I don't mean design a cover in bright clashing colors just to draw eyeballs. What I mean is, take a risk to do things slightly differently. Look at what your competitors are doing, use similar concepts, but put your own trademark on it. Take your design a bit further, make it edgier and sexier.

3. Be consistent

Unless your book topics are radically different from each other, I'd suggest creating some kind of consistency. Get a look that suits your image and then weave elements of it into your book cover designs. This clean cut uniformity contributes to the professional look of your book page and creates familiarity in the minds of your readers. You could do this by sticking to certain font styles, complimentary colors, or using the same illustrator or designer each time.

Hire a professional designer

The difference between an amateur book cover and a professional book cover is immediately obvious. Unless you have killer design skills yourself, rather hire a designer to help you out. He'll have valuable knowledge and will save you hours of sweat, tears and self-doubt. Just be sure to draft up a very detailed and concise brief, including examples of covers you like, beforehand so he understands your direction fully.

If you find someone who gets it right, stick with him. I found mine through a referral from a friend.

What I've learned

Above is the cover from one of my best selling books so far: "Your First $1K. How to Start a Successful Blog and Make Money Doing It". You can see the title is very large, it has a character and style to it, and the graphics and colors are simple and bold.

Chapter 5

How to Craft the Perfect Book Description for Amazon

Would you order "fried crap" off a restaurant menu?

I was catching up with my friend the other day. He just got back from a huge trip to South East Asia and he was telling me about his adventures, the parties, and the delicious food.

One story he told me really got us going:

"One day I was walking down the street and a restaurant smelled so good I had to go inside. They handed me a menu, and what do I see in big bolded letters on the first page? *"Fried Crap!"*. I didn't eat there."

Fried Crap!?

We shared a chuckle. Turns out it's not so uncommon for people in Cambodia to confuse 'B' and 'P', so the fried crab on the menu lost its appeal.

So, what's this got to do with Amazon descriptions? Everything, actually.

Books are just like restaurants. But instead of food, people consume content.

As an author, it's your job to make sure your readers get excited about your book. You need to set the stage properly that triggers their emotions, leaving them eager to buy and start reading.

See, sometimes people are going to buy your book without thinking much. Sometimes they're just going to stumble upon your book randomly and want to try it out, just like my friend and the Cambodian restaurant.

But instead of glancing at a menu, what do potential customers look at? What's the last step before they make a decision? Your description.

Now, I'll be honest. Until summer 2015, I didn't pay much attention to my Amazon book descriptions. I just provided a quick summary, copied and pasted something from my conclusion, and called it a day. Amazon descriptions can be up to 4,000 characters (usually around 600-700 words), and I kept mine under 2,000 characters.

Then, I realized my mediocre Amazon descriptions probably weren't helping my book sales, rather they were hurting them. In late October 2015, one of my books (http://amzn.to/1R4znTx) became a #1 best seller. I doubt that ever could have happened with a lousy description...

Your Amazon book description is your last chance to make the sale (http://business.tutsplus.com/articles/how-to-write-an-ebook-description-that-sells--fsw-39539). It's an opportunity to force the reader to think, *"I need this book right now"*.

So, how do you do that? See my top 11 tips below.

11 Ways to Improve Your Amazon Descriptions Today

1.Don't Make It About Yourself

You don't need to include how many awards you've won and why you're so awesome. Instead, make it about the reader. What are they going to learn from your book? Why is it going to be worth their time and money?

2. Be Exciting

A boring description will make the reader believe the book (and probably the author) is boring. Enough said. Your description should be lively and fun to read. If you're not getting the reader pumped to read your book, then it's not exciting enough.

For example, if your book is about weight loss, then your description should be getting the reader excited to lose weight. You can get them excited by laying out how great they're going to feel when they reach their weight loss goals. Another great way to do this is to...

3. Paint a Picture with Benefits

After reading *Your First $1k,* you will:

+ Know how to avoid writer's block and get passed blank page syndrome

+ Make sure your content gets in front of the right people

+ Overcome any fears or roadblocks that are keeping you from taking your blog to the next level

+ Know the best strategies on how to make your first $1,000 in passive income

+ Learn how to use guest blogging to grow a huge email list

+ Get access to 2 more free ebooks that deliver more value than you'll be able to handle

Don't just talk about what's inside the book and what problems your readers face, take it a step further and show the readers what life will be like once they follow your advice. Always be honest though.

For example, in my book, "Guest Blogging Masterclass", instead of saying, "You will learn how to get more guest blog posts," I say, "You'll be able to grow your blog and generate massive traffic through guest blogging".

4.Target Keywords

Search terms		Avg. monthly searches	Competition	Suggested...	Ad impr. s...	Add to plan
seo for beginners		1,000	Medium	$3.76	--	»
seo 101		880	Low	$30.29	--	»
seo for startups		110	High	$14.30	-	»
seo for entrepreneurs		-- --		--	--	»

If people aren't searching for the keywords, then no one is going to find it. Do some keyword research and see what people are searching for, both on Amazon and Google. Then include those keywords in the descriptions (http://janefriedman.com/2015/04/02/amazon-book-description/). Having keywords that people are searching for can actually increase your chances of being found. Just make sure that when they do find you they are not turned off by your keyword stuffing instead of an inspiring description.

5. Start Strong

Screw up the first line and you've lost the reader and perhaps a potential customer. The first line is your first impression. It needs to draw people in and pique their interest. A good first line should be short and easy to read. A lot of successful Amazon sellers start with a question that resonates with the reader. For example, in my book, *"How to Find Time to Write"* (http://www.amazon.com/How-Find-Time-Write-Overcome-ebook/dp/B010QPAVV6), I start with a few questions that resonate with my target audience (see screenshot below).

See all formats and editions

Kindle
$0.00 kindleunlimited

Subscribers read for free
$0.99 to buy
✓*Prime* Borrow for free ▾

Have you always **wanted to write more,** but you could **never get started?**

You kept putting it off, hoping you'd eventually find some free time, only to find out that months or even years went by and **you saw zero progress?**

Another great way to start is by including a solid value proposition of what the customer can expect after reading the book. The example below demonstrates that. It explains in the first line that the reader will "master the fundamentals, hone your business instincts, and save a fortune in tuition."

6. Write Sales Copy

"But it's a description, not a sales pitch!"

Your book is a product and you are trying to sell it.
This calls for sales copy. True, it may cost only 99
cents, but you still have to convince the reader that
it's worth it.

Your description should not be a summary or a bio,
it's a sales page. If you're not confident writing sales
copy, then hire someone
(http://www.jeremyginsburg.com/amazon) to do it for
you. It's not cheap, but the ROI is worth it.

7. Write The Problems in the Language of Your Readers

If you can define your reader's problem better than
they can, they're going to trust that you have the best
solution. Your goal here is for people to read your

description and think, *"Wow, that's me! How can this guy/girl read my mind?!"*

8. Enhance the Style

Add effects to your description (https://kdp.amazon.com/help?topicId=A377RPHW6ZG4D8) by using **bold**, *italics*, underlines, UPPER CASE, and different sized titles. Not only does this make it more interesting and allow you to display more emotion, but it also makes it easier to capture the attention of someone who is browsing quickly and not reading it word for word. Make it eye-catching, but don't go overboard. See an example below:

Do you feel trapped sometimes? Do you want to clear your mind and find your purpose?

This booklet will add more freedom and happiness to your life. It could change your life too.

"If you want to break free and live life on your terms, while doing work that makes a difference and adds value to other people's lives. Then you should read this book." SA – verified purchase review.

We are all freer than we think we are

9. Make it clear

If the reader can't tell exactly <u>what the book is about</u> http://catherineryanhoward.com/2012/10/05/the-11-ingredients-of-a-sizzling-book-description/ () by the description, there's a small chance he/she is going to read it. Avoid being too fancy and be sure you stay on topic. Also make sure you include what the book is about and not just why people should buy it. See the example below for a weak Amazon description.

10. Proofread.

Yeah, it's a no brainer, but screw this up and you can kiss your potential sale goodbye. It may be best to hire a proofreader to look for typos or grammar issues with fresh eyes. I recommend sites like <u>Upwork</u> (https://www.upwork.com/) to find affordable professionals.

11. Include a Call To Action

Imagine you've got a killer description that hooks the reader in but when they read until the end, because you're missing a call to action, they browse around, look at other reviews and end up getting distracted. That's a missed opportunity for a sale.

The most effective way to include a call to action is to write something along the lines of, "now, scroll to the top of this page and buy the book and get started today." Don't think of it as being salesy, rather you're just encouraging them to take action.

Scroll to the top and click the "buy now" button, and kiss your days of writer's procrastination goodbye.

▲ Read less

Length: 62 pages ▾   Word Wise: Enabled ▾   Matchbook Price: $0.00
What's this? ▾

*Optional: Including testimonials. This can go both ways. On one note, a testimonial will rarely hurt you. On another note, it could screw up the flow of your copy.

Having testimonials is optional. It can be helpful but not all successful books on Amazon have them.

I've chosen not to include testimonials in mine because I don't have any from people with credentials. But if Mark Cuban or James Altucher (http://www.jamesaltucher.com/) left me a 5 star review, you bet I'd include that in my description!

See all 2 formats and editions

Kindle	Paperback
$9.99	$18.42

Read with Our **Free App**   30 Used from $8.69
29 New from $13.27

"This is a must read for all startups and stakeholders."
— **Steve Blank**, author of The 4 Steps to the Epiphany, creator of **Customer Development** methodology

"The Entrepreneur's Guide is an easy read. It is written in a conversational tone, doesn't take itself too seriously, and avoids extraneous fluff."

— **Eric Ries**, Author & Creator of the **Lean Startup** methodology
Read more

So, there you have it. The good news is now you know what you need to get more sales from your Amazon books. The bad news? It may take some time and extra effort. But it's worth it.

Chapter 6

How to Get More Email Subscribers by Self-Publishing on Amazon

Building a book business without building an email list is like building a house without a foundation. I made this mistake (http://mfishbein.com/mistakes-passive-income-business/) when I first started my business and had to learn quick to prevent my company from crumbling around me.

But I did, I learned fast, and now I can help you build your list (http://mfishbein.com/first-100-email-subscribers/) right from the beginning.

An ever increasing, engaged e-mail list is the driving force behind any great online marketer. And, as self-published authors, our e-mail subscribers can equate to continual customers, which means more sales for our books.

Attracting one time visitors to your site or your book is like filling a leaky bucket with water. They'll look around, hopefully buy a book or two, and then likely move on and never return. The bucket never fills, meaning your pockets never do either.

A much better business model is to convert traffic into continual paying customers. This can be tricky though, so how do I do it? I use e-mail marketing to build my list and continue providing value to my subscribers through autoresponders and ebook offers.

This is a highly effective strategy to increasing your customer lifetime value and boosting book sales. I'll walk you through exactly how to do it below.

The journey from reader to subscriber to lifelong customer

To start, it's helpful to understand, from the customer's perspective, what process they go through from discovering our book up to subscribing to our email list.

First they find our book, this is usually either by:

1. Searching or browsing Amazon

Customers Who Bought This Item Also Bought

The Morning Routine Blueprint: How to Wake Up Early, Energized and ... Mike Fishbein
⭐⭐⭐⭐⭐ 16
Kindle Edition
$2.99

Your First $1k: How to Start a Successful Blog and Make Money Doing it ... Mike Fishbein
⭐⭐⭐⭐⭐ 17
Kindle Edition
$2.99

The Happy Life: 21 Principles for Energy, Excitement, and Wealth in ... Chad Grills
⭐⭐⭐⭐⭐ 1
Kindle Edition
$0.99

Pain Management: Change Your Posture Change Your Life (Get Pain Free) Your ... Greg Parry
⭐⭐⭐⭐⭐ 31
Kindle Edition
$2.99

Stupid On Purpose: The Art of Ignoring Good Advice, Doing Whatever The Heck ... Mark Messick
⭐⭐⭐⭐⭐ 24
Kindle Edition
$2.99

2. Promotions outside of Amazon (eg. Buckbooks)

3. Through content marketing, such as blog posts, slideshare, guest posts, etc

Once they have found your book, they purchase it and read it. While reading, they see a link to a free ebook you have written, providing more information or further steps. This incentivizes them to give you their e-mail address in order to download it. Remember, you can't just expect their details without providing value in return.

They click on the link through to the landing page where they sign up to receive the free ebook. This adds value to the reader and another e-mail address to your growing list. Now that they are on your list you can send them future promotions, updates, content etc.

To streamline my process, I set up autoresponders (http://mfishbein.com/autoresponders/) so my readers continue to recieve content and book sales promotions without me spending anymore time.

How to convert your readers into email subscribers

1. Create a squeeze page

I recently switched to LeadPages (http://www.leadpages.net/) to optimize my landing pages for conversion. LeadPages makes it really simply to create landing pages that not only look good but convert as well.

2. Offer an ebook as additional value and an incentive to sign up

This is a very effective strategy for collecting email addresses. Provide something of value to incentivize them to sign up.

I've synched LeadPages to ConvertKit so when visitors enter their details on my squeeze page, they're automatically added to ConvertKit too.

ConvertKit automates the whole process of hosting the ebook and sending it to the subscriber for me. Subscribers get an email like the one below to download the pdf:

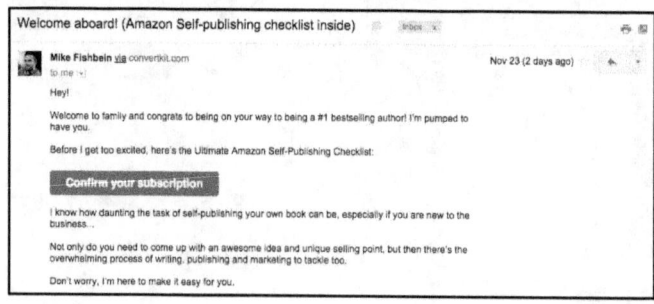

3. Make it compelling with copywriting and design

Even if you're offering your ebook for free, you still need to lure potential readers in with great copywriting and design. If your writing skills aren't up

to it, hire a writer through Upwork
(https://www.upwork.com/) to help you out. On the
design side, I use Fiverr (https://www.fiverr.com/) to
create a 3D cover of the book I am offering.

I will make 3D book cover

$5

4. Create an autoresponder course

This way, readers continue to get offers and value
without you spending any more time.

✉ #4 Content marketing

A 3 day course with 2 emails.

124   44.9% 17.1% 7

SUBSCRIBERS   OPEN RATE   CLICK RATE   UNSUBSCRIBERS

I've created personalized courses according to what they signed up for. So, if they sign up for my ebook on guest blogging, they receive emails that contain advice on guest blogging. They also get links to blog posts I've written where they can learn more, along with sales copy to buy my book.

I include a "soft sell" banner image at the bottom of most emails.

I JUST WROTE A NEW BOOK:

Your First Bestseller

It's all about self-publishing a successful book. It's packed with everything from positioning your book so it sells to marketing it to sell even more. I'd love to give you all my best strategies.

Just click on the button below.

TELL ME MORE !

MIKE FISHBEIN

YOUR FIRST BESTSELLER

HOW TO SELF-PUBLISH A SUCCESSFUL BOOK ON AMAZON

5. Engage with your audience

Autoresponders are a great tool for asking customer development questions (http://mfishbein.com/customer-development-questions-create-content/) so you can create even better content. In my welcome e-mail I include my customer development questions and encourage readers to respond with any topic-related questions they might have too.

Here are a couple examples of questions I like to ask:

- What's the biggest question you have about xyz?
- What's your biggest struggle when it comes to xyz?

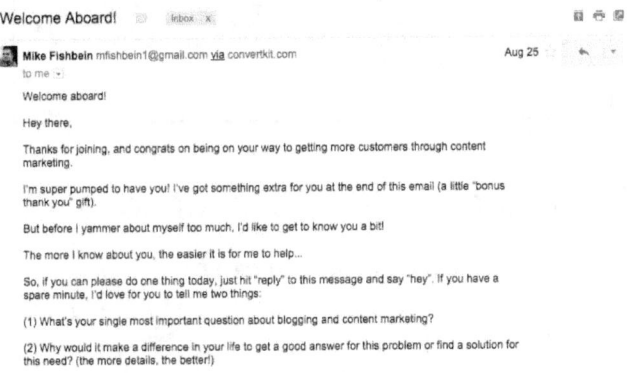

6. Link to the squeeze page from within the book

Now that you have your landing page and autoresponder sequence set up it's time to place a link to your landing page in a place where they will see it. In the introduction of my book, I add a link to the free ebook under a subheading called "Additional Resources." I link to it again in the conclusion of the book under a subheading called "Next Steps."

Want more traffic and customers? Does blogging on your own domain ever feel like you are farting in the wind?

Guest blogging has been one of the best ways I've increased traffic to my blog and boosted my SEO ranking. In this book, you will learn the step-by-step process I use to get published on top sites to help you grow your site through guest blogging. Guest blogging is a great way to grow your audience, especially in the early stages.

Get the book for free here.

7. Track clicks and conversions

If you're using ConvertKit, you can do this by appending ?ref=YourCampaignName to the landing page URL to create a new campaign. Alternatively, you can use Bitly, the Wordpress plugin, PrettyLink, install Google Analytics on your page, or use the analytics provided by Leadpages or your preferred provider.

Key Takeaways

Self-publishing on Amazon (http://mfishbein.com/how-to-self-publish-a-book-on-amazon/) is a great way to reach more potential readers and customers. By converting readers into email subscribers you can continue to sell to them on your own accord. Offering a free ebook provides value and offers an incentive in exchange for their email addresses. Once you start building your list you can use autoresponders to reach readers directly, increasing your reach and your book sales.

Make your book awesome and market it right

Write an awesome book jam-packed with value, and readers will be excited to read more books by you. Use an effective marketing strategy to get your book in front of as many people as possible. We'll learn more about what specific book marketing strategies to use in Part 3.

Chapter 7

How To Title Your Book: A Step-by-Step Guide to Keyword Research

So you've written your book. Congratulations! But how do you make sure that shoppers on Amazon want to buy it and read it?

With a little research, you can increase the likelihood of people finding your book simply by including the terms and words that they are already searching for. It's a small and simple step, but it's an important one. There are over 300,000 shoppers on Amazon. By improving your ability to rank on the search engine, you'll get a lot more book sales.

In this post, I'll show step-by-step exactly how I did keyword research for my Amazon Kindle book that ended up being a #1 bestseller.

Writing and marketing a book is important, but doing keyword research also plays a big role in the book's success. If you brainstorm some keywords and phrases, browse Amazon for other books that are doing well, analyze the results and split test the titles, you'll find it's much easier to self-publish a #1 bestseller.

1. Brainstorm keywords

Step one is to simply brainstorm a list of 10+ keywords that are relevant to your book topic. For this example, my book is about morning routines, being productive, and maximizing energy. Not all the keywords are going to be great ones, so just writing down as many as you can may be a better move.

For me, my initial keywords I thought up were: morning routine, morning ritual, morning procedure, morning productivity, wake up earlier, and successful morning.

2. Browse Amazon for relevant books

The point of this process is to look and see what books are already selling well so you don't have to reinvent the wheel. You do this by browsing Amazon and looking at the books that are selling well.

My book was about morning routines, so I wanted to look at other books on that topic. To do this, I simply searched Amazon using the keywords I came up with in step #1.

3. Analyze the successful books

Next, I analyzed the books that came up in the searches. I did this mostly by looking at the last category in the pictures below: "Amazon Best Sellers Rank".

Any book with a rank below about 75,000 is worth considering.

Product Details

File Size: 438 KB
Print Length: 172 pages
Page Numbers Source ISBN: 0979019710
Simultaneous Device Usage: Unlimited
Publication Date: December 7, 2012
Sold by: Amazon Digital Services, Inc.
Language: English
ASIN: B00AKKS278
Text-to-Speech: Enabled
X-Ray: Enabled
Word Wise: Enabled
Lending: Not Enabled
Enhanced Typesetting: Not Enabled
Amazon Best Sellers Rank: #2,037 Paid in Kindle Store (See Top 100 Paid in Kindle Store)

> #6 in Kindle Store > Kindle eBooks > Nonfiction > Self-Help > **Spiritual**
> #6 in Kindle Store > Kindle eBooks > Business & Money > Entrepreneurship & Small Business > **Entrepreneurship**
> #15 in Books > Business & Money > Small Business & Entrepreneurship > **Entrepreneurship**

If the book is ranking high, it means people are buying it.

Based on my judgment, I found a few books that appeared to be doing well. It's a pretty small niche, so I only found a few.

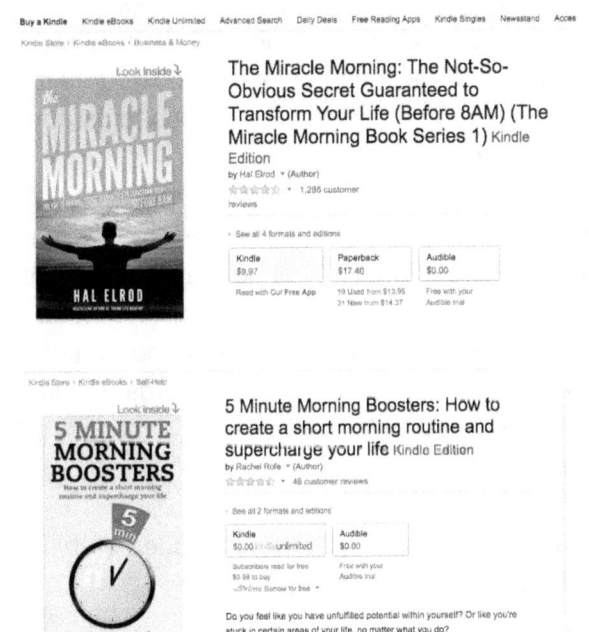

The point is to see what kind of language these books are using.

On top of keyword searching, analyzing your competition also helps you get ideas and inspiration for cover design inspiration. These books are performing well for a reason, so it's important that you notice what's working.

4. Gather a list of new terms to analyze

Now that you've researched your competition, it's time to add to your previous list with new keywords. Use your personal judgment based on your taste for your audience and how that compares to the topics of your book.

Make sure to find a balance between search friendly (traffic) and personal (conversion). Loading it with keywords does not help if the title doesn't make sense. For example, a title like "Morning routine ritual wake up" has a bunch of great keywords, but it would make a horrible title because it doesn't make sense.

Here are some of the new terms I added at this step (most were secondary terms).

<u>Primary Keywords</u>

morning routine
wake up
morning ritual
routine
morning routines

<u>Secondary Keywords</u>

Morning Boosters
Supercharge Your Life
Wake up Successful
Increase Your Energy
How to Increase Your Energy
How To Wake Up Early
Wake Up Early
Stop Being Lazy
Gain Massive Motivation
Organize Your Life
Transform Your Life

5. Analyze Keyword Traffic

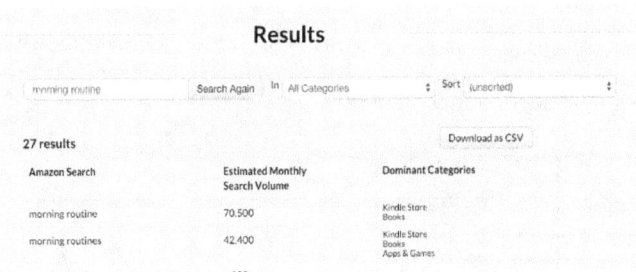

Amazon Search	Estimated Monthly Search Volume	Dominant Categories
morning routine	70.500	Kindle Store Books
morning routines	42.400	Kindle Store Books Apps & Games

I pay for an account with Merchant Words (https://www.merchantwords.com/) in order to analyze Amazon searches. You can also use Google's Keyword Planner. It's pretty easy, you just enter the term and it shows you many searches it gets per month. This book is sold on Amazon, but I also want to rank on Google too. Plus, if people are searching for these terms on Google, there's a high change the results will be similar on Amazon.

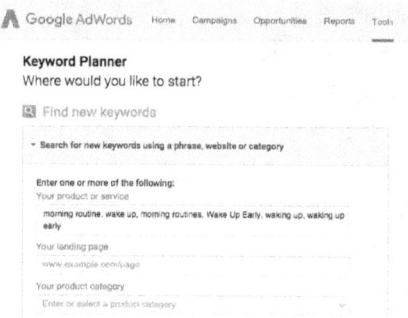

Here were the results for my keywords. I've highlighted the high search volume terms in green, medium volume in yellow, and low volume in red. It's also important to keep in mind relevance and competition.

Primary Keywords:

morning routine - 70.5k
wake up - 298.5k
morning ritual - n/a
routine - 134.5k
morning routines - 42.4k

Secondary Keywords:

morning boosters - n/a
supercharge your life - n/a
wake up successful - n/a
Increase Your Energy - 1.6k
How to Increase Your Energy - <100
How To Wake Up Early - <100
Wake Up Early - 9.5k
Stop Being Lazy - 15k
Gain Massive Motivation - n/a
Organize Your Life - n/a
Transform Your Life - 6k
how to organize your life - 35.2k

You can also use the "Keyword Ideas" section to generate more related keywords that are related to your niche. Once you do that, you'll get a set of new keywords.

When I did that, I got more new ideas:

Keyword (by relevance)		Avg. monthly searches	Competition	Suggested bid	Ad impr. share	Add to plan
how to wake up early		22,200	Low	$0.01	–	»
benefits of waking up early		1,000	Low	$0.02	–	»
tips for waking up early		590	Low	–	–	»
keep waking up early		260	Low	–	–	»
i hate waking up early		320	Low	–	–	»
waking up too early		1,300	Low	–	–	»
my morning routine		9,900	Low	$0.03	–	»
how to sleep early and wake up early		320	Low	–	–	»
ways to wake up early		260	Low	–	–	»
how to wake up		12,100	Low	$0.84	–	»

Here are some of the additional words that were recommended

waking up - 142.5k
morning rituals - 500
routine - 18.5k (not very relevant because it can be about any routine)
waking up early - 8.5k
how to stop being lazy - 4.8k (this is red because it's not really relevant to my audience)
organizing your life - 6.4k

Now we have some solid inspiration, so let's...

6. Brainstorm 3-5 titles and 3-5 subtitles

Now it's time to use the data that you've collected and come up with some ideas for your book. Make sure not to rip someone off, your book title should be original. First, do a brain dump and write out as many titles as you can.

If you're not sure how to do this, set a timer to ten minutes and just write until the time is up. Then, do the same thing for subtitles. Once you have a list of over ten for each, go back and pick your 3-5 favorite titles and subtitles.

A great title accomplishes two things. You want it to include keywords that people are already searching for, but you also want your title to catch people's attention.

On top of that, your title has to hook in the reader (http://www.thebookdesigner.com/2015/11/derek-doepker/). It has to make them think, "oh my god, I NEED to read this and I need to read it now."

Your title needs to grab their attention. You can do this by adding controversy, humor, benefits, surprise, or novel ideas. You also want to make sure your title includes benefits for the readers. What are they going to learn? What end result are you selling them?

Lastly, you have to make them care. Why would they pick your book over someone else's? What's so special about this book? To hit on this point, think about what people care about: ease, comfort, speed, saving money, pain avoidance, etc.

Now with this in mind, keep your prioritized keyword list on hand so you can check them off when it's used in a title/subtitle. Here's mine:

morning routine
wake up
Wake Up Early
How to Wake Up Early
morning routines

waking up
waking up early
how to wake yourself up
how to wake up
my morning routine
morning ritual
morning rituals

I'm pretty set on using the morning routine keyword in the title because of the volume and relevance and it's still aesthetically pleasing. I came up with a few variations.

Here are some of the titles I came up with:

Morning Routine Success Plan
Morning Routine Blueprint
Morning Routine Master Plan
The Morning Routine Blueprint
The Morning Routine Master Plan

Next, I repeated the same process with subtitles:

How to Wake Up Early and Increase Your Energy Everyday
The Secrets to Waking Up Energized and Motivated Everyday
Lifehacks to Wake Up Early, Energized and Motivated Everyday
How to Wake Up Energized and Motivated Everyday
How to Wake Up Early, Energized and Motivated Everyday

How to Create Your Most Productive Morning
How to Wake Up Early and Get More Done Before
8AM

The last time is to create a finalized list of about three to five combinations that you love.

Morning Routine Success Plan: How to Wake Up
Energized and Motivated Everyday
The Morning Routine Master Plan: How to Wake Up
Early and Get More Done Before 8AM
The Morning Routine Blueprint: How to Wake Up
Early, Energized and Motivated Everyday
Morning Routine Success Plan: How to Wake Up
Early and Get More Done Before 8AM
The Morning Routine Master Plan: How to Wake Up
Early, Energized and Motivated Everyday

7. Split test on Mechanical Turk or Pick Fu

Now you've got your ideas and it's time to let research do the work for you. There are many sites you can do this on, I've used Mechanical Turk (https://www.mturk.com/mturk/welcome) and Pick Fu (https://www.pickfu.com/) in the past. Both sites are simple to use and not too expensive.

Option A

Pimp Your Book: How to Self-Publish a Bestseller on Amazon

卌 卌 l

WINNER

Option B

Your First Bestseller: How to Self-Publish a Book on Amazon and Make Money Doing It

卌 卌 卌 卌 卌 卌 lll

Instructions→

Judge the sentiment expressed by the following item toward: The most engaging and attractive title for a book on Amazon

The Morning Routine Blueprint: How to Wake Up Early, Energized and Motivated Everyday

Average Sentiment rating of 0.75 based on **20 responses**

Strongly Positive (+2)	(1)
Positive (+1)	(1)
Neutral (0)	(1)
Negative (-1)	(0)
Strongly Negative (-2)	(0)

Based on your results, you either have a clear-cut winner, or you don't. If you don't, you can perform more polls based on what worked.

Here were my two clear winners:

The Morning Routine Blueprint: How to Wake Up Early, Energized and Motivated Everyday
Morning Routine Success Plan: How to Wake Up Energized and Motivated Everyday

Personally, I like the first one more because I'm not a fan of using the word "success", but that's just me!

Here's how the book did during the launch:

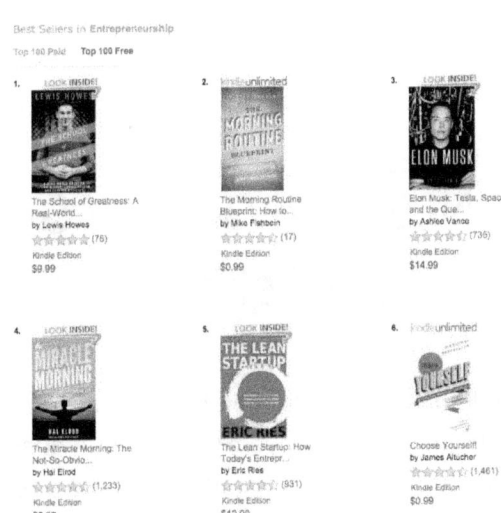

#2 in entrepreneurship category isn't so bad! Especially since I'm pretty sure Lewis Howes went on several national TV shows and podcasts to promote his book and I went on...zero. It ranked #1 in other categories, so I'm not complaining! :-)

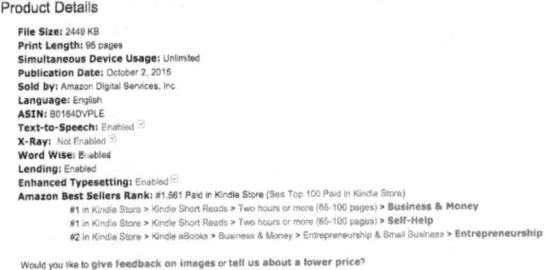

Product Details

File Size: 2449 KB
Print Length: 95 pages
Simultaneous Device Usage: Unlimited
Publication Date: October 2, 2015
Sold by: Amazon Digital Services, Inc
Language: English
ASIN: B0164DVPLE
Text-to-Speech: Enabled
X-Ray: Not Enabled
Word Wise: Enabled
Lending: Enabled
Enhanced Typesetting: Enabled
Amazon Best Sellers Rank: #1,561 Paid in Kindle Store (See Top 100 Paid in Kindle Store)
　　#1 in Kindle Store > Kindle Short Reads > Two hours or more (86-100 pages) > **Business & Money**
　　#1 in Kindle Store > Kindle Short Reads > Two hours or more (86-100 pages) > **Self-Help**
　　#2 in Kindle Store > Kindle eBooks > Business & Money > Entrepreneurship & Small Business > **Entrepreneurship**

Would you like to give feedback on images or tell us about a lower price?

This book continues to rank high and sell well, and I know doing all of this keyword research helped. So, I hope it helps you as well!

Part 2

The Nuts and Bolts of Self-Publishing

You've got all your assets. You have book content that people are going to love and you have design and marketing assets that will make people eager to buy. Now is the time to publish!

Part 2 provides tutorials and best practices for Amazon KDP (Kindle), Createspace for paperback, and ACX for audiobook.

This part is very practical. I suggest you create accounts and log in to complete these actions as you read. If you are not yet ready to publish your book, and want to learn more about how to market your book, you may want to skip to Part 3.

The following chapters are step-by-step guides to publishing your book in multiple formats, including best practices along the way.

Chapter 8

How to Self-Publish a Kindle Book on Amazon

Kindle Direct Publishing (KDP) makes it incredibly easy to publish Kindle ebooks to Amazon. Your book will appear in the Kindle Store within about a day and be available to people all around the world. It's completely free and you get up to 70% royalty on sales. Publishing takes less than 5 minutes and you can make changes to your book at any time after it's live.

You don't have to be a Shakespeare or Stephen King to be an author these days and you don't have to battle with pesky publishers to get your book out there either. I've gone through the process over 12 times now and captured every step to help show you how to self-publish a book. Follow these steps below, and you will have self-published your own book by the end of today.

Step 1: Visit kdp.amazon.com and Sign In or Sign Up

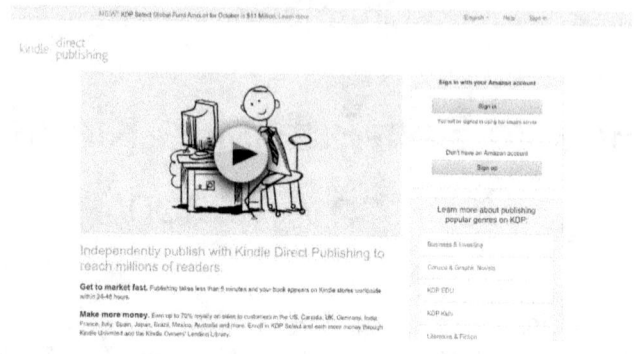

To get started, first create an account with Amazon Kindle Direct Publishing (https://kdp.amazon.com/). Or simply sign in if you already have one. Then, visit your Dashboard (http://kdp.amazon.com/dashboard).

Step 2: Add New Title From Your KDP Dashboard

Click on "Create new title". This will bring up the "Introducing KDP Select" screen below.

Step 3: Enroll in KDP Select

Introducing KDP Select

Take advantage of KDP Select, an optional program that makes your book exclusive to Kindle and eligible for the following benefits:

- **Reach more readers** - With each 90-day enrollment period, your book will appear in Kindle Unlimited in the U.S., U.K., Italy, Spain, Germany, France, Brazil, Mexico, Canada and India and the Kindle Owners' Lending Library (KOLL) in the U.S, U.K., Germany, France, and Japan which can help readers discover your book.
- **Earn more money** - Earn your share of the KDP Select Global Fund when customers read your books from Kindle Unlimited and the Kindle Owners' Lending Library. Plus, earn 70% royalty for sales to customers in Japan, India, Brazil and Mexico.
- **Maximize your sales potential** - Choose from two promotional tools including: Kindle Countdown Deals, time-bound promotional discounts for your book, available on Amazon.com and Amazon.co.uk, while earning royalties; or Free Book Promotion, where readers can get your book free for a limited time.

Learn more

☑ **Enroll this book in KDP Select**

By checking this box, you are enrolling in KDP Select for 90 days. Books enrolled in KDP Select must not be available in digital format on any other platform during their enrollment. If your book is found to be available elsewhere in digital format, it may not be eligible to remain in the program. See the KDP Select Terms and Conditions and KDP Select FAQs for more information.

I do this with all my books and have seen great benefits. It enables me to offer my book for free for a selected period after publishing, which encourages Amazon to promote it further and helps me build my email list (http://mfishbein.com/first-100-email-subscribers/). You can learn more about KDP Select here.

Step 4: Enter Your Book Title and Subtitle

Enter in your book name and subtitle. Tell your readers what your book is about so they know what they will get out of reading it. For bonus points, use keywords that your readers are searching for to increase your chances of being found. Here are 5

<u>more tips</u> (http://www.inboundpro.net/naming-an-ebook/) for naming your book.

Step 5: Enter Your Book Description

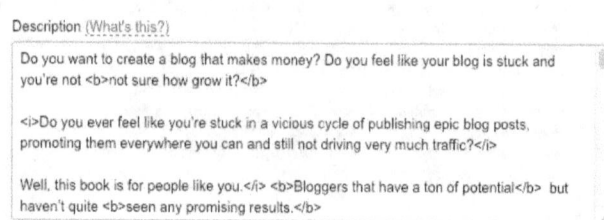

This is your readers' first real taste of your book's content, like the blurb on the back cover of a printed book. Make sure it is well written, interesting and informative enough to give your readers a good idea of what your book is about. You can use <u>some HTML</u> (https://kdp.amazon.com/help?topicId=A1JPUWCSD 6F59O) to make your description more engaging.

Step 6: Enter Book Contributors

Click on the "Add contributors" tab to add yourself as an author.

Step 7: Add Author Name

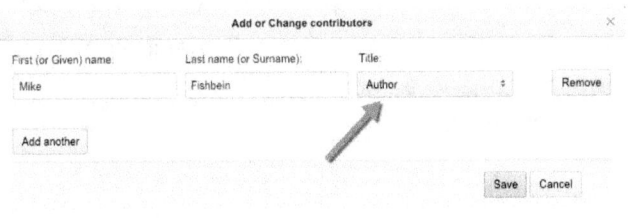

Add in the author's name—that's you! This can be a pen name if you like.

Step 8: Verify Your Publishing Rights

2. Verify Your Publishing Rights

Verify Your Publishing Rights (What's this?)
○ This is a public domain work.
◉ This is not a public domain work and I hold the necessary publishing rights.

As author, you own the publishing rights to your book, click here to verify that.

Step 9: Target Your Book to Customers

3. Target Your Book to Customers

Categories (What's this?)

Add Categories

You can choose up to two categories for your book. Choose these carefully as they help your intended readers to find your book. I usually decide on the categories based on competing books that are performing well.

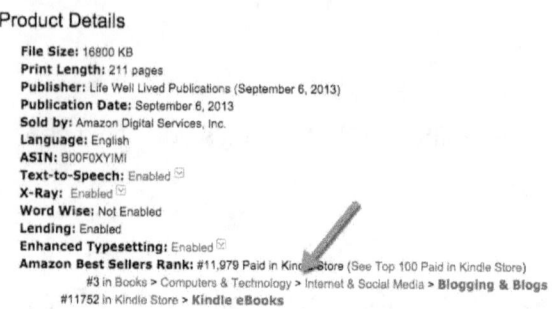

This is where a book's category ranking is shown.

Step 10: Choose Categories

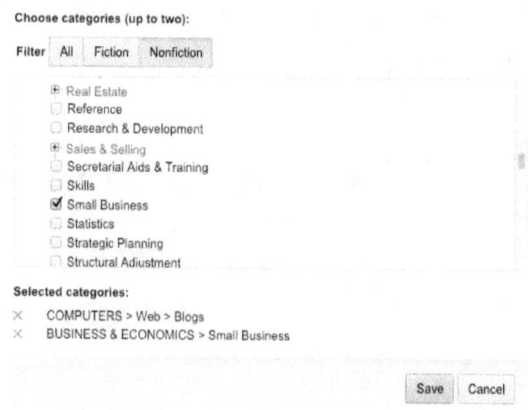

The more specific the niche your category falls into, the more likely it will be found by the right people.

Step 11: Select Age Range if Applicable

Leave ages blank unless it is a children's book.

Step 12: Select Search Keywords

Search keywords (up to 7, optional) (What's this?)

Grow Your Blog, monetize your blog, Blogging for Profit, How to Blog for Profit, Make Money B|

0 keywords left

Search keywords help your book to be found by people who are searching Amazon for relevant topics. I choose these keywords based on merchant words, Google Keyword Tool and competitors.

Step 13: Select Your Book Release Option

4. Select Your Book Release Option

Please select if you are ready to release your book immediately or if you would like to make it available for pre-order (What's this?)

(●) I am ready to release my book now
(○) Make my book available for pre-order

There's no time like the present so make your book available immediately! You can make changes to it at any stage after publishing if needs be.

Step 14: Upload or Create Your Book Cover

Your cover image says as much about your book as your title does. You can create your own using their cover creator but it won't be nearly as attractive as having one designed by a professional designer.

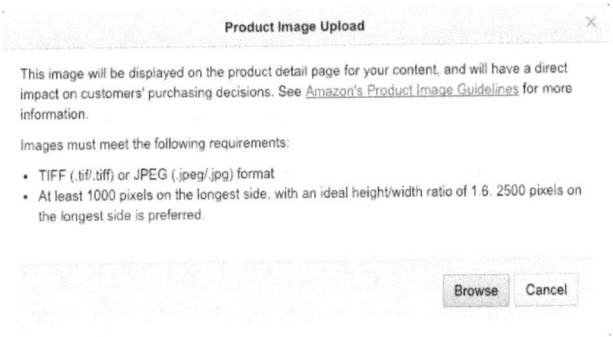

To display optimally, read the guidelines to ensure your image is in the required formatting.

Step 15: Cover Uploaded Successfully

5. Upload or Create a Book Cover

Upload an existing cover, or design a high-quality cover with Cover Creator. (optional)

I have a book cover designed and ready to upload
Please read our Cover guidelines

Browse for image...

I want to design a cover using the Cover Creator (beta).

Launch Cover Creator

✓   Cover uploaded successfully.

Step 16: Select a DRM option

6. Upload Your Book File

Select a digital rights management (DRM) option: (What's this?)
○ Enable digital rights management
◉ Do not enable digital rights management

If you click on "What's this?" you can learn more about digital rights management (DRM). You will see a window that looks like this:

Digital Rights Management

DRM (Digital Rights Management) is intended to inhibit unauthorized distribution of the Kindle file of your book. Some authors want to encourage readers to share their work, and choose not to have DRM applied to their book. If you choose DRM, customers will still be able to lend the book to another user for a short period, and can also purchase the book as a gift for another user from the Kindle store.

Important: Once you publish your book, you cannot change its DRM setting.

Essentially, DRM determines if your readers are permitted to lend your book out to others.

Step 17: Upload Your Book File in The Correct Format

Book content file:

Browse

> Learn more about Kindle content creation tools for children's books, educational content, comics and manga.
> Learn KDP content guidelines> Help with formatting

If you need help with how to format your book correctly read this (https://kdp.amazon.com/help?topicId=A2GF0UFHIY G9VQ), or go ahead and upload it in one of the following:

 Word (DOC or DOCX) (https://kdp.amazon.com/help?topicId=A2GF0UFHIY

G9VQ#word)

[HTML](https://kdp.amazon.com/help?topicId=A2GF0UFHIY) (ZIP, HTM, or HTML)
(https://kdp.amazon.com/help?topicId=A2GF0UFHIY
G9VQ#zip)

[MOBI](https://kdp.amazon.com/help?topicId=A2GF0UFHIY) (MOBI)
(https://kdp.amazon.com/help?topicId=A2GF0UFHIY
G9VQ#mobi)

[ePub](https://kdp.amazon.com/help?topicId=A2GF0UFHIY) (EPUB)
(https://kdp.amazon.com/help?topicId=A2GF0UFHIY
G9VQ#epub)

[Rich Text Format](https://kdp.amazon.com/help?topicId=A2GF0UFHIY) (RTF)
(https://kdp.amazon.com/help?topicId=A2GF0UFHIY
G9VQ#rtf)

[Plain Text](https://kdp.amazon.com/help?topicId=A2GF0UFHIY) (TXT)
(https://kdp.amazon.com/help?topicId=A2GF0UFHIY
G9VQ#plain)

[Adobe PDF](https://kdp.amazon.com/help?topicId=A2GF0UFHIY) (PDF)
(https://kdp.amazon.com/help?topicId=A2GF0UFHIY
G9VQ#adobe)

[Kindle Package Format](https://kdp.amazon.com/help?topicId=A2GF0UFHIY) (KPF)
(https://kdp.amazon.com/help?topicId=A2GF0UFHIY
G9VQ#kpf)

Step 18: Converting Book to Kindle Format

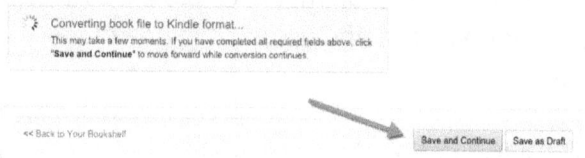

Once your book has been converted, click "preview" to see if it has converted properly. This is a crucial step if you have more complex formatting like tables and graphs.

Step 19: Verify Your Publishing Territories

Your First $1k

Step 1	Step 2	Optional
Your book	**Rights & Pricing**	**KDP Select Benefits**
Almost there. Waiting for file conversion..	¦ Not Started...	

8. Verify Your Publishing Territories
Select the territories for which you hold rights: (What's this?)

⊙ Worldwide rights - all territories
○ Individual territories - select territories

FAQs

How do I identify my territorial rights?
If you hold worldwide rights, choose

Verify whether you have the rights to distribute your book worldwide or only in certain territories.

Step 20: Set Your Pricing and Royalty

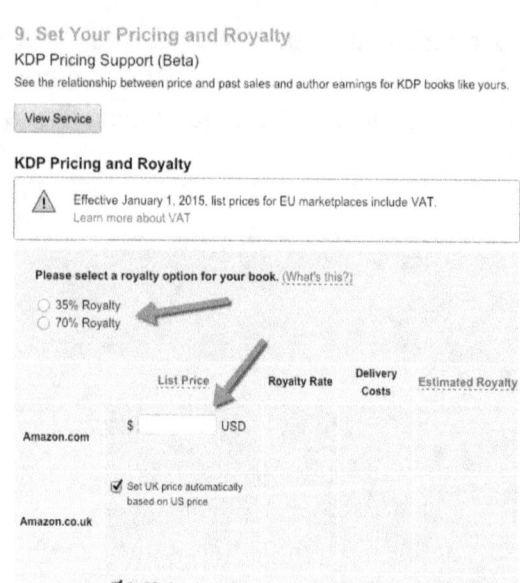

9. Set Your Pricing and Royalty

KDP Pricing Support (Beta)

See the relationship between price and past sales and author earnings for KDP books like yours.

View Service

KDP Pricing and Royalty

⚠ Effective January 1, 2015, list prices for EU marketplaces include VAT.
Learn more about VAT

Please select a royalty option for your book. (What's this?)

○ 35% Royalty
○ 70% Royalty

	List Price	Royalty Rate	Delivery Costs	Estimated Royalty
Amazon.com	$ _____ USD			
Amazon.co.uk	☑ Set UK price automatically based on US price			

Select your pricing dependent on your goals and marketing/ sales funnel. Here's some more info to help you make the right choice:

List Price Requirements
(https://kdp.amazon.com/help?topicId=A301WJ6XCJ 8KW0)
Sales and Royalties FAQ
(https://kdp.amazon.com/help?topicId=A30F3VI2TH1 FR8)
Pricing Page
(https://kdp.amazon.com/help?topicId=A29FL26OKE 7R7B)

Step 21: Enroll in Kindle Matchbook

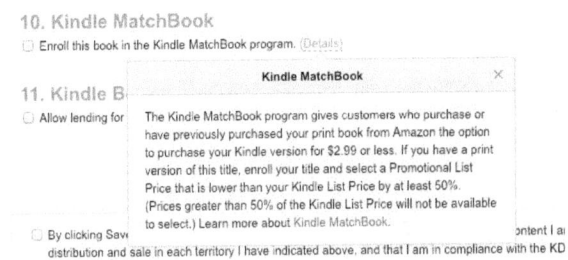

Selecting this means that readers who've already bought the print version of your book, get a discount on your Kindle version. This is a good incentive to help hang on to those recurring customers.

Step 22: Select Kindle Book Lending

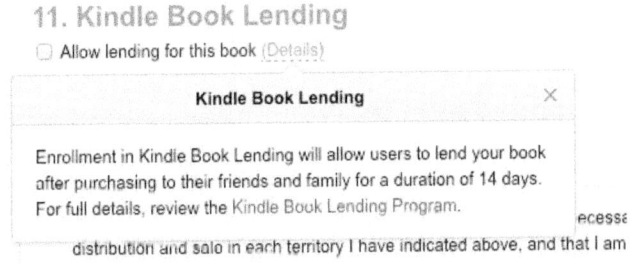

Selecting this means readers can lend your book out for 14 days. This helps spread the word about your book and bring in more buyers.

Step 23: Check All the Boxes

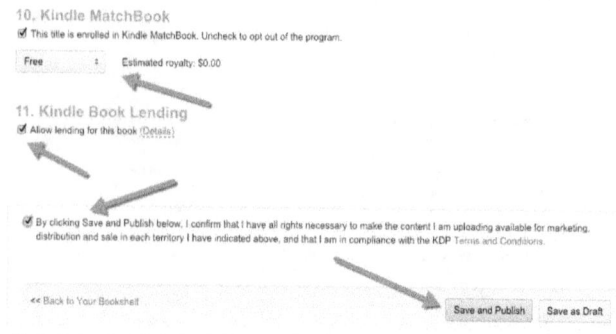

I suggest you select both Kindle MatchBook and Kindle Book Lending. Agree to the terms and conditions and then click "Save and Publish."

Step 24: Publishing

Within 12 hours your book will be live on the world's largest bookstore! It's just that easy. Next we'll cover how to create a paperback book using Createspace and an audiobook using ACX.

Chapter 9

How to Self-Publish a Paperback Book with Createspace

As self-published authors, it's important that we build a professional image to differentiate us from the thousands of others ebook authors out there. One of the ways I do this is by converting my Kindle books into paperbacks using Createspace (https://www.createspace.com/). Not only does this improve the professional image of my book page, it also allows me to reach a whole new market who may not own a Kindle, or who just prefer the old school experience of holding and reading a paperback. A bigger audience means a potential boost in sales.

Although I still get more sales through Kindle, being able to indicate that I am a paperback, and audiobook, as well as a Kindle author, really improves my credibility and professional image. Viewing my author page, readers can immediately see I'm not just another self-published author offering just another Kindle book.

Converting your Kindle book to print version using Createspace is a simple process if you know what you are doing. Fortunately I have done this many times before so I am here to help you along the way. I've written this quick and easy step-by-step guide to help you take your ebook from digital format right through to an ink and paper book you can hold in your hands.

In a nutshell, the process includes: formatting your book cover for Createspace specifications, formatting your book for paperback, and uploading it through Createspace per their qualifications.

Before starting you'll need your finalized book in digital format, a good idea of what you want to put on the cover, a clear marketing strategy, and of course, an account with Createspace.

Got all of that ready? Then let's get started.

Step 1: Use Upwork to find a book formatter

Format Word Doc for Createspace Paperback Publishing

Other - Admin Support   Posted 1 day ago

🖋 Fixed Price   Ⓢ $35 $$ Intermediate Level
                            Budget   I am looking for a mix of
                                         experience and value

To start, you need to hire a formatter to convert your book's content to Createspace format. Upwork (https://www.upwork.com/) is a great place to find a book formatter at an affordable price.

Step 2: Enter in a brief description of your job

Details

I have a Google/Word Doc of my book. I need it to be formatted to be published on CreateSpace.

Must have previous job doing this work.

More info here:

https://www.createspace.com/en/community/docs/DOC-1482

https://www.createspace.com/Products/Book/InteriorPDF.jsp

http://www.brandonmdennis.com/createspace-formatting/

Must have strong attention to detail and good formatting ability.

Other Skills: Document Conversion   eBooks   Format & Layout   Google Docs
Microsoft Word   PDF Conversion

There are a lot of formatters on Upwork, so you don't need to enter in a very detailed description of your requirements. Above is a screenshot of what I include.

Step 3: Create a book cover for Createspace

I will convert amazon kindle to createspace book cover

$5

Before you upload to Createspace, you'll need both a book cover and a book file. You can either use Fiverr (http://www.fiverr.com/) to convert your Kindle book cover to a Createspace cover, or have your Kindle designer do it for you.

Step 4: Start a new project on Createspace

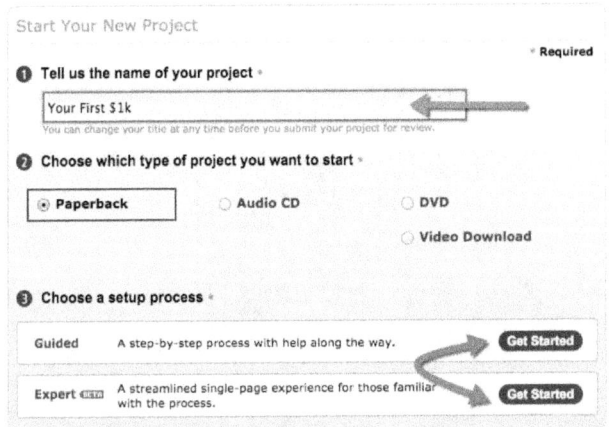

Now you are ready to upload your book. Head over to Createspace (https://www.createspace.com/) and log in to get started. Enter in your book title, select paperback format and choose either the guided or expert setup process based on your level. I choose the "Expert" process as the "Guided" process doesn't actually make it much easier.

Step 5: Upload your book cover to Createspace

Once you have got your cover back from Fiverr, provide feedback if you require more changes or, if you're happy with it, download it as pdf to upload to Createspace.

Step 6: Enter all book information on Createspace

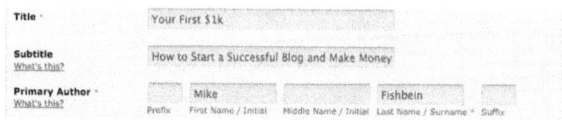

Enter all the relevant information for your book such as title, subtitle, author, description and categories.

It's best to just use your Amazon book description to describe your book. Here's an example of mine below.

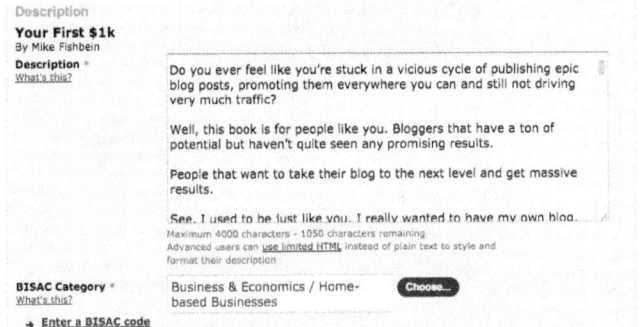

Step 7: Submit for review

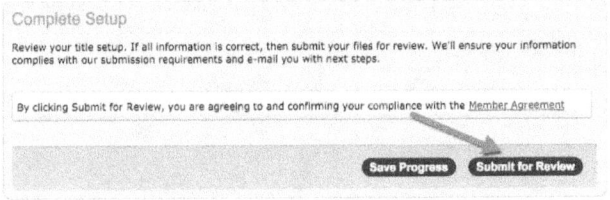

After you've entered all the information needed for the cover and interior of your book, submit it to Createspace for review.

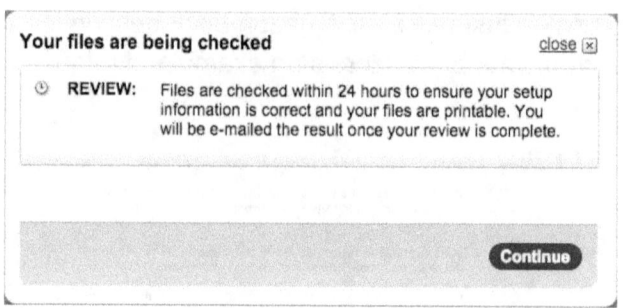

Your files are now under review and Createspace will get back to you within the next 24 hours. Once it is ready, you'll then have the chance to either order a physical copy or view online for publishing

Step 8: Receive email accepting interior and cover files

You will receive an email from Createspace once your interior and cover files have been accepted. You are now ready for a final review.

Step 9: Proof your book

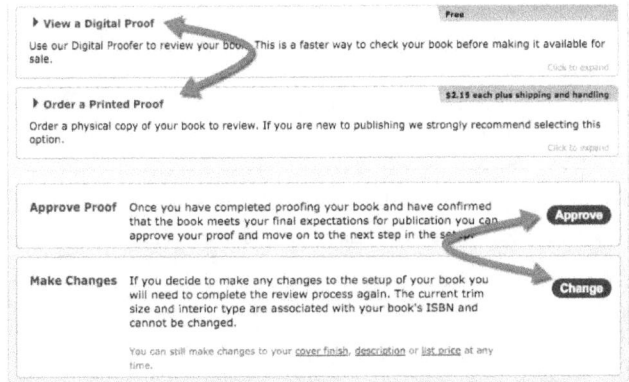

You can choose to either proof your book in digital or physical format. Once you have reviewed it, click "change" to make changes if necessary, and then "approve" once you are happy and ready to move on to the next step.

Step 10: Your setup is now complete

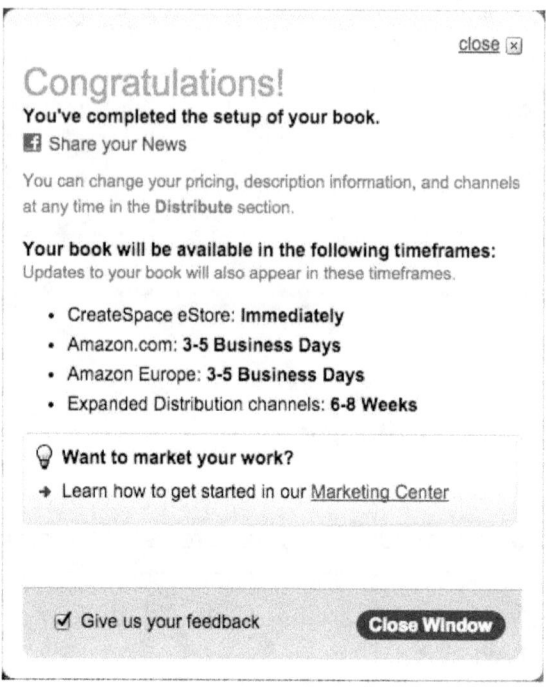

Once your book has been improved, it will immediately be live on Createspace. You will need to wait a bit longer for it to be available on Amazon.

Your book is now live! Remember to go back to your Createspace dashboard to check your royalties and watch the passive income roll in!

Chapter 10

How to Create an Audiobook Using ACX

The ebook marketspace is getting more crowded by the day and it's increasingly difficult to stand out. It doesn't matter how good your books are, there's a lot of fish, both big and small, to compete with.

One of my solutions to drawing a wider audience is to turn my ebooks into audiobooks. Doing this helps me to tap into a whole new audience on Audible who, otherwise may never even have heard of me, adds more versatility to my current products, and boosts the professional image of my book pages.

I now reach more people than ever before and am able to serve a whole new sector of potential customers who prefer listening to audio over reading.

Creating audiobooks boosts the professional image of your book on Amazon, not to mention, you get a $50 bounty from Amazon if yours is the first audiobook an AudibleListener member buys. So far I've sold over 3,000 audiobooks and have earned over 30 bounties.

In this post I will walk you through the whole process of how to create an audiobook using ACX. I've captured and detailed every step involved from converting your book to auditioning and working with the best narrator for the job. By the end of reading this you will be well on your way to reaping the benefits of a whole new market space. Log in now and follow along as you read.

Step 1: Go to <u>www.acx.com</u>

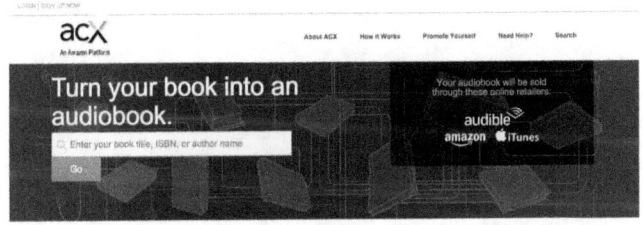

Log in or sign up at <u>www.acx.com</u> and enter in either your book title, ISBN, or author name. Amazon will then search Amazon.com for rights you might have using your name.

WHAT TO DO NOW

- **Claim your book** only if you have the rights.
- **Create an ACX profile** for this book. This will attract narrator auditions, so try to make it compelling and specific. Tips for creating a title profile.
- **Have multiple projects?** Select only 5 or fewer to receive auditions to ensure successful productions. See why.
- **Wait for auditions** to come in or proactively search narrator samples now. What do I look for in an audition or sample?
- **If you're narrating your own book or already have completed audio files**, make sure you review our Audio Submission Requirements first to avoid any delays in getting your audiobook on the market.

If this is your first audiobook or even if you have created a few already, ACX provides some very helpful guidelines to get you started. Read them to get an idea of the process.

Step 2: Select Your Book

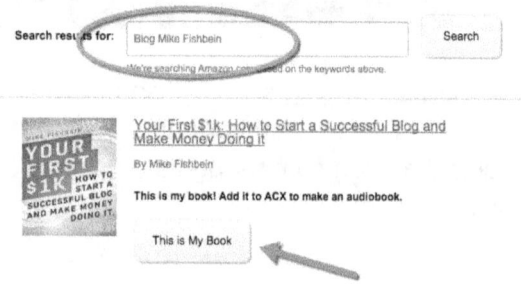

Select the book you'd like to turn into an audiobook.

Step 3: Choose the best narration option for you

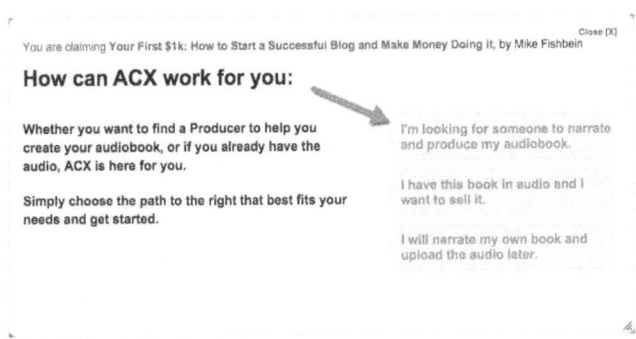

Here you get to choose whether you are looking for a narrator, have already converted you book into audio and just wish to sell it, or if you will be doing the narrating yourself. I outsource my production so I select the first option.

Step 4: Agree to the terms

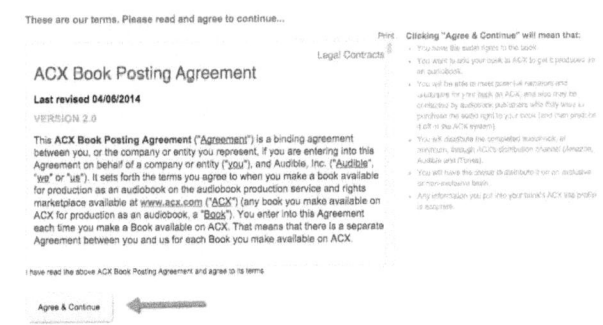

Read through ACX's book posting agreement

carefully before continuing. Each time you turn a book into an audiobook using ACX, you enter into a separate agreement.

Step 5: Enter your book description

About my book:

> Do you want to create a blog that makes money? Do you feel like your blog is stuck and you're not sure how to grow it?
>
> Do you ever feel like you're stuck in a vicious cycle of publishing epic blog posts, promoting them everywhere you can and still not driving very much traffic?
>
> Well, this book is for people like you. Bloggers that have a ton of potential but haven't quite seen any

(835 characters remaining)

Provide potential Audible listeners with information about your book, giving them a sense of the content and value for readers. It's best to just use your Amazon book description for this.

Step 6: Enter your copyright information

Copyright Information:

This information will be read within the credits of the audiobook and it will also display on our retail sites when the audiobook is on sale. This information is optional at this time, but you will need to provide it by the time you send the manuscript to the Producer.

Print Copyright Owner Name:	Mike Fishbein
Print Copyright Year(s):	2015
Audiobook Copyright Owner:	Mike Fishbein

Note: This is initially an optional field, but will need to be provided by the time you approve the first 15 minutes of your production. The copyright information will be read by the Audiobook Producer in the credits section of the book.

Confirm yourself as copyright owner for your original

book as well as for your audio book. For the copyright year, enter in the current year.

Step 7: Select a category

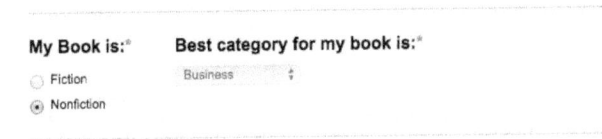

First indicate whether your book is fiction or nonfiction and then select the category most suited to your book.

Step 8: Specify narrator voice

Here is where you specify what type of narrator voice you want. Give some careful consideration to tone, accent and gender as this will influence how readers interpret your message. For my books I tend to stick to the above requirements.

Step 9: Add in additional comments

Additional comments:

> Author has self-published over 12 kindle books, 6 audiobooks, and sold over 2,500 audiobooks to date. Audience for book is beginning and aspiring bloggers. It contains clever strategies and tactics for growing successful blog and monetizing it.

(1752 characters remaining)

Here's your chance to provide directions or advice to Producers who may audition for this book. It is also a good place to make your book as appealing as possible to ACX Producers. For example, you can include marketing information, selling points, best-seller status, awards, foreign language translations and reviews. Additionally, please include information about the Author's reach and fan-base (i.e. 5,000 followers on Twitter, 6,000 fans on Facebook).

Add in additional comments that give narrators a good indication of who you are, your accolades, the value of your book, and who your target readership is. Get narrators excited to collaborate with you!

Step 10: Add an audition script

Audition script:

By providing an audition script, Producers will be able to supply you with their best performances for your work. Please choose to upload your audition script or type in the audition script. You must provide only a small excerpt of your book.

Audition Script Notes:

> I've spent hours and hours on posts that barely got any views. Other times, a post that I spent 20 minutes on blows up.
>
> Learn as you go. Get stuff out there and see what works. You can read about new concepts and ideas all you want, but by not doing anything, you get nowhere

Choose audition script file from your computer:

You can upload Word, PDF or TXT files.

Browse

If you have trouble uploading your file, you can input your audition script as text.

Save & Continue

Either type in or upload an audition script to get the best narrator fit for your book. Do you want to hear how well they tell stories? How captivatingly they retell facts or data? Can they get your unique sense of humor across? Choose a script which will give you a good sense of the narrator's scope.

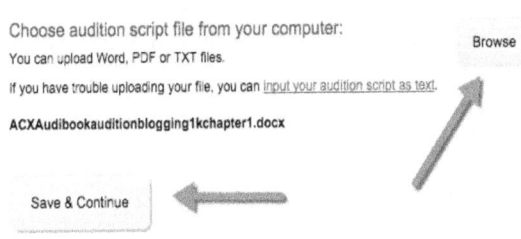

If you prefer, you can upload your script. Make sure it is in either Word, PDF or TXT format.

Step 11: Enter your book's word count

Once you enter your book's word count, you have finished the first section of how to create an audiobook using ACX and we are on to next: Distribution. This is where you will set the parameters for the distribution of your audiobook. To start, type in your book's word count.

Step 12: Specify your territory rights

What territory rights do you own?

As a rights owner for this title, you are entitled to specific distribution area rights. Please check your contract so that you can identify what territory rights you own to distribute your audiobook for the language in which you post the title.

World

Unless you have a limitation on the areas your book is allowed rights within, select "World". Choosing this means you have permission to sell your audiobook in every country.

Step 13: Select payment method

How would you like to pay for the audiobook's production?

You can pay the producer a per-finished-hour fee (Pay For Production) or you can simply share royalties with them (Royalty Share). If you are unsure at this time you can click both options, but the more specific that you are, the more likely you are to find the right Producer for you. You can always change your mind; you don"t need to commit 100% until you are ready to make a formal offer to one of the Producers you find on ACX. To learn more about these two options, please check out the What's the Deal? section.

Choose one or both below:*

☑ **Royalty Share** (50-50 share of royalties earned)

50-50 share of royalties earned. By choosing this method of payment, you will be paid monthly by ACX based on half of royalties earned each time the audiobook sells. This limits your potential revenue, but also limits your risk. **Learn more.**

Distribution will be EXCLUSIVE distribution on Amazon, Audible, and iTunes ™

(40% royalty) Why does it have to be exclusive?

☑ **Pay for Production**

I'll pay: $ $100-$200 PFH ⬍   Per finished hour
(1.6 hrs @ $$100 - $$200 PFH hr = $NaN - $NaN)

Select how you wish to pay your ACX narrator. You can choose either a revenue share model or a pay-per hour production fee. If you are unsure which one you want, select both for now and make a final decision once you have secured a suitable narrator.

Step 14: Select distribution type

Choose between exclusive or non-exclusive. I prefer the exclusive option. The royalty percentage is higher and I prefer to have all my books and audiobooks sold in one place.

What type of distribution do you want?

◉ **Exclusive** distribution through Amazon, Audible and iTunes (40% royalty)

If you choose Royalty Share option above, your audiobook must be exclusive to ACX. Under this model, ACX has the exclusive right to distribute the audiobook. If you choose this option, the audiobook cannot be distributed by any entity except ACX in any market or format.**Why?**

○ **Non-Exclusive** distribution (25% royalty)

Your audiobook will be sold through Amazon, Audible and iTunes via ACX, as well as wherever else you choose. Under this model, you can grant distribution rights to parties other than Audible in any market and any format. **What's the Deal?**

To learn more about these options, please check out What's the Deal?

Save & Continue

Next, click save and continue to move on to the final section in the process.

Step 15: Review and post

 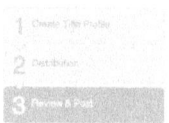

Your First $1k: How to Start a Successful Blog and Make Money Doing it
By Mike Fishbein

Estimated Length: 1.6 hours
Project Budget: Royalty Share or $100-$200 PFH
Word Count: 15,291

Language: Distribution: Exclusive
Territories: World

Ok, now we are on to the third and final step of creating an audiobook using ACX: Review and post.

Click "Post to ACX" so narrators can pick up your script and start auditioning for your audio book. The sooner you do this, the better!

Step 16: Review auditions

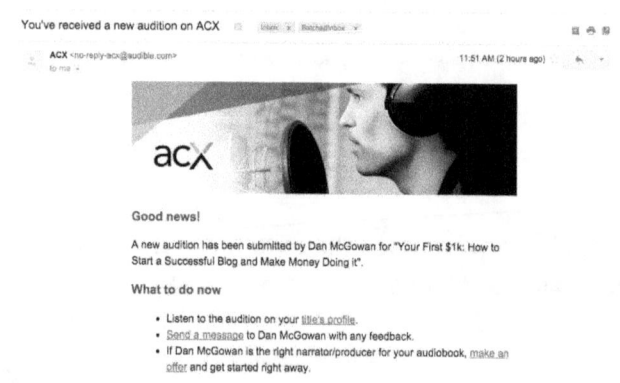

Now comes the fun part; narrators will start auditioning for your audiobook. You will receive an email notification each time a new audition comes through. I usually wait about 5 days to let them come in. If you have a specific narrator in mind, you can invite them to audition for your book.

Step 17: Click on New Auditions

To listen to the auditions, log in to your ACX profile and click "new auditions' in the top menu bar.

Step 18: Listen to unheard auditions

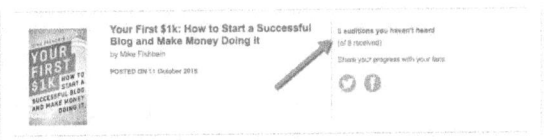

You will find all the auditions you haven't listened to yet in the right sidebar.

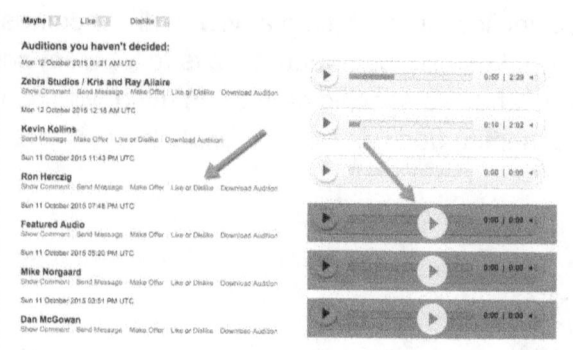

The listening process is simple on ACX. Click on the play button to listen to the audition and then click either "like" or "dislike" depending on your preference.

Step 19: Set your schedule

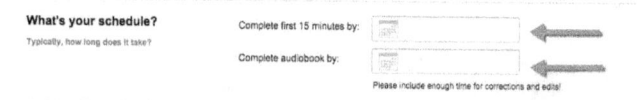

Once you have decided which narrator you want to use, and alerted them, set your schedule to indicate what timeframe they have to work within. This must include edits and correction time.

Step 20: Choose a payment method

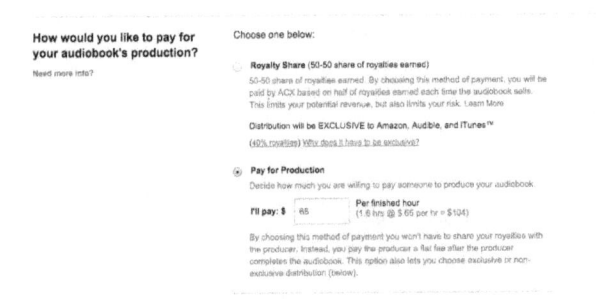

This is where you decide whether to choose a royalty share or pay for production method. So if you were previously unsure and selected both, this is when you will need to make your decision. Discuss it with your narrator to see what suits both of you best.

If you're paying, you have to coordinate with your narrator and most likely pay via PayPal. If you select the royalty share option, ACX will handle it.

Before you send your payment proposal off, click "preview" to check it's correct.

Step 21: Send offer

Once you are happy with your payment proposal, click "send offer" to send it off to your narrator.

Step 22: Send your narrator the manuscript

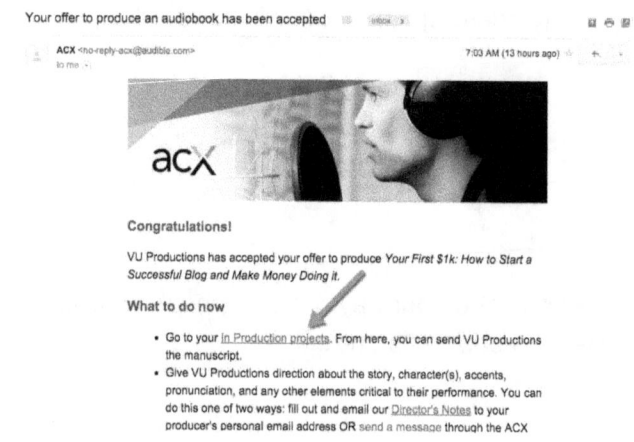

Once your narrator has accepted your offer, the first

step in your collaboration is to send them the manuscript for your audio book. Click "In Production projects" to bring up the tab below.

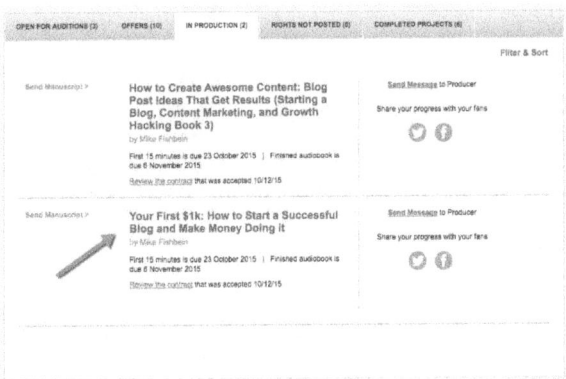

Here you can select the manuscript you wish to send your narrator. Click on the title and then click browse to upload it. Your manuscript must either be in Word, PDF, or TXT format.

Your manuscript will then have been sent to your narrator. Now you need to wait for them to review it and record the first 15 minutes which they will then upload for your approval.

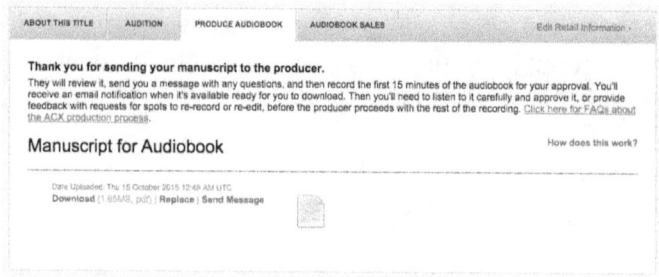

Step 23: The first 15 minutes are ready for you to hear

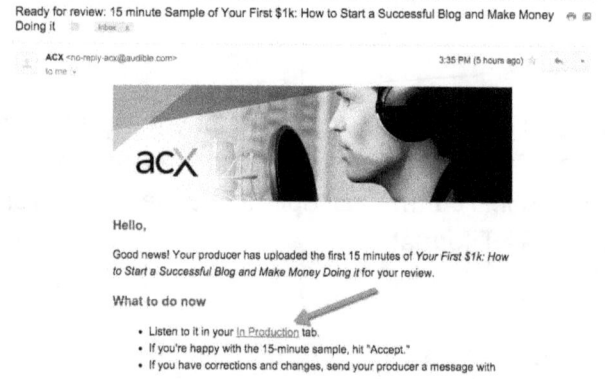

Your narrator will review your manuscript and record the first 15 minutes of your audiobook as a sample for you to listen to. You will receive an email notification when it is ready for you.

Step 24: Listen to the first 15 minutes

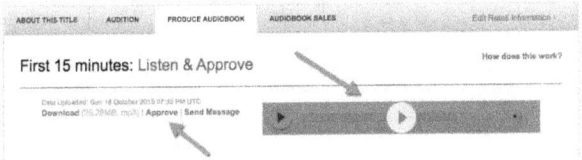

Click "play" to listen to the recording and select "approve" if you are happy with it. If you have queries or concerns about it, you can click "send message" to contact your narrator.

Once you have listened to the recording and clicked "approve", sit back and relax. You will need to wait for your narrator to finish recording the rest of your audiobook. You can check the "produce audiobook" tab to see if any files have been uploaded.

Step 25: Create or upload your cover

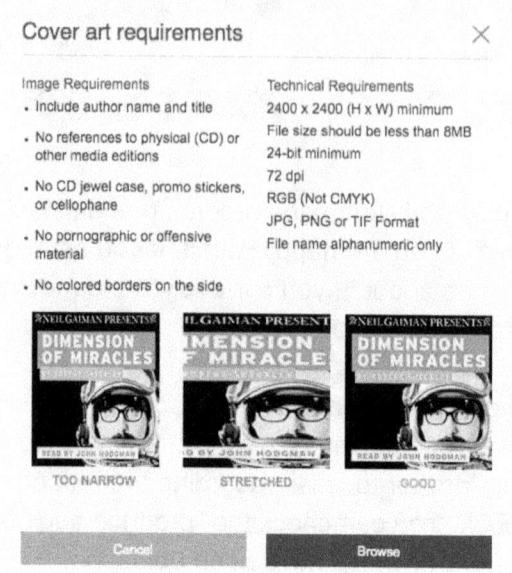

While you are waiting for your narrator to finish recording your book, you can create your audiobook cover. The image and technical requirements can be seen above.

Step 26: Covert book cover to ACX format

I will convert 2 book covers to ACX or 3D formats

$5

I use Fiverr to convert my cover images to ACX format.

Step 27: Upload cover art

Once I have converted my image and saved it to my computer, I click here to upload my cover image.

Step 28: Do a final review

You will receive an email notification when your audiobook is ready for a final review. Click on the link to open it up.

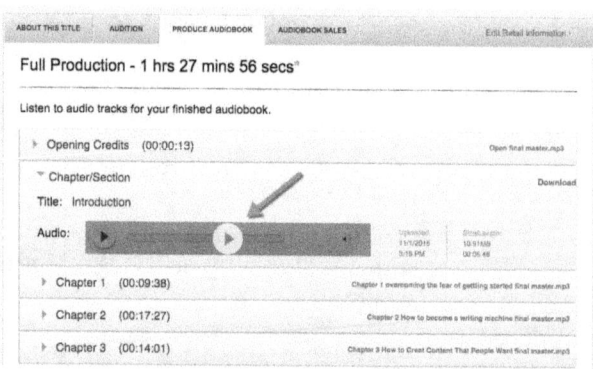

Listen to each chapter separately by pressing the play button on the track you want to hear. If you're not quite satisfied with it yet, you can request more changes from your narrator.

Your First $1k: How to Start a Successful Blog and Make Money Doing it
By Mike Fishbein

Estimated Length:	Project Budget:	Word Count:
1.6 hours	565.0 per hour	15,291

Language:	Distribution:	Territories:
English	Exclusive	World

Cover art requirements

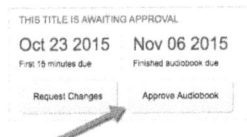

THIS TITLE IS AWAITING APPROVAL

Oct 23 2015   Nov 06 2015
First 15 minutes due   Finished audiobook due

Request Changes   Approve Audiobook

Otherwise, if it's good to go, click "approve audiobook".

Step 29: Wait for the quality assurance checks

What happens now

- Your audiobook will pass through **both ACX and Audible** quality assurance (QA) checks.
- Once it passes, we will let you know and begin distributing it on Amazon, Audible and iTunes. The whole process usually **takes up to 10-14 business days**, as long as there are no problems.
- If your audiobook does not pass QA for any reason, you and your producer will be contacted right away with instructions for how to remedy this.
- Meanwhile, confirm your bank information is up to date so you can start receiving your royalty payments.

Once you have confirmed the audiobook, you will receive an e-mail with the above information. This clearly lays out what the next steps will be. You just have to confirm your bank information and wait.

Step 30: Your audiobook is now live

A week or two later, you will get an email confirming that your audiobook is now live on Amazon and Audible!

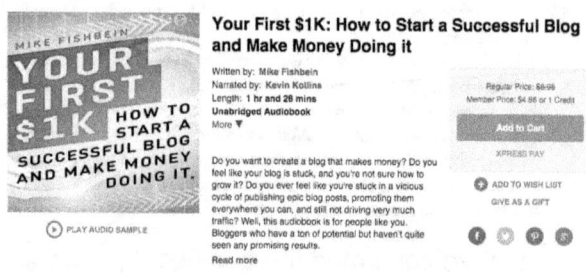

Once your audiobook is live, make it a habit to regularly check back to your dashboard to see how your sales are doing.

Key Takeaways

Turning your ebooks into audiobooks is a great way to stand out in an overcrowded market. You can reach a whole new marketspace of Audible listeners and cater to customers who prefer listening to audiobooks rather than trying to make time in their busy schedules for reading. Providing both ebooks and audiobooks (and paperbacks too!) boosts your professional image as an author and adds another stream to your passive income.

Part 3

Book Marketing: How to Sell More Books

So you've written a book that readers will love and positioned it so that when they find it they will be eager to buy it. Now you need more people to find it.

Part 3 of this book covers one of my favorite parts of self-publishing, and one of the most important: book marketing!

This part is all about how to drive large quantities of relevant traffic to your book.

We will cover Amazon KDP ads, paid promotion sites, content marketing and guest blogging, email marketing, and how to get Amazon to promote you to their shoppers.

When you're first starting out, it will be hard to drive large volumes of traffic to your book on your own. Thus, Amazon will be one of your best sources of traffic. Not only can Amazon be one of the easiest ways to get traffic, it can be one of the best.

To get Amazon to promote your books, you need to get a large volume of downloads in a short amount of time. So, I recommend you coordinate all of the marketing strategies discussed below within the first week of publishing your book.

There are a lot of moving parts to marketing a book. It can be helpful to visually map out your launch and marketing strategy, create a to-do list with everything you need to get done, and schedule it all so that you get it done at the right time.

Chapter 11

How to Get Amazon to Promote Your Book for You

Amazon is the biggest bookstore in the world. As a beginner author, your current audience probably pales in comparison to Amazon's hundreds of thousands of active shoppers.

Thus, one of your best channels for acquiring readers will not be your external channels (such as your email list, content marketing, etc), but Amazon itself.

To understand how to get Amazon to promote your book, we must understand how Amazon works and what their incentives are…

Amazon has many different businesses and types of products, but we will focus on its book business.

As a company with shareholders, Amazon's ultimate goal is to make money. It makes money by selling books.

Their incentives are therefore aligned with yours: to

sell books.

However, Amazon needs to consider both the short-term and the long-term.

To maintain a sustainable business it must provide value to its customers by providing them with **_high quality books_**. If they sell their customers crappy books, customers will not be happy and they will not come back.

But Amazon could not possibly have a team of people that reads every book to see what it should recommend. Instead, it has an algorithm, based on metrics that indicate whether the book is quality or not.

So, by improving these metrics we can encourage Amazon to promote our book to their customers.

What would indicate to Amazon that a book is high quality? Here are a few indicators:

- Reviews
- Downloads
- Relevance to what shoppers are searching for

By gaining understanding for these factors and how we can improve them, we can quickly increase our sales…

Reviews

Reviews show Amazon that people like your book. If people like your book, they will want to promote it to their audience.

There are "verified purchase" reviews and "non verified purchase" reviews. A non-verified purchase is more likely to be fake, so Amazon is more likely to remove, or de-value, the non-verified purchase.

Thus, use free promotion days to give your book to friends, family, and other authors to read and write a review.

How many reviews is enough? Amazon does not disclose much information about how their algorithm works exactly, but authors are sharing their experiences to provide data as to what works. I can't give you an exact number recommendation, but based on my experience and the conversations I've had with other successful authors, at least 10 positive reviews is a good start.

Action items:
- Ask your friends and family to download and review your book
- Network with other authors to exchange honest reviews
- Make sure your book is awesome so that readers will review it organically

- Ask for a review at the end of your book
- Ask for a review in an email to your list

Downloads

When Amazon notices that a lot of people are downloading a given book, it indicates that their customers are finding the book valuable. If their customers are finding the book valuable, it is in their best interest to promote the book to even more of their customers.

Thus, getting a large number of downloads in a short amount of time, and consistently for several days, can give you an exponential boost in book sales.

The following chapters will cover how to drive traffic to your book so that you can get more downloads.

Action items:
- Get a large amount of downloads during the first week of your book launch
- Continue to drive sales to show consistency
- Read the next chapters to learn how to accomplish the above :)
- If you don't have a large audience or email list, consider using KDP Select free days

Relevance

Amazon is in some ways like Google in that people use it to search for what they need. In Google's case, users are often searching for free information. In Amazon's case, they are searching for paid products.

By positioning your book so that it is relevant to your target audience and what they are searching for, you can increase the number of people who find you through Amazon.

In addition, Amazon books tend to rank fairly well on Google. So by using keywords that people are searching for on Google, you may be able to acquire more readers through Google.

Action items:

- Do keyword research to determine what your target audience is searching for
- Use those keywords in your title, subtitle and description

During launch

Once you hit publish, it's time to really get your marketing ball rolling. This is a critical time, as getting a lot of downloads consistently over the first few days and weeks of your launch, signals to Amazon that they should be promoting it to their users.

Publish your book on book promotion sites

Rather than just promoting your book on your own platforms, use paid book promotion sites to get the word out. By publishing my book on Buck Books I managed to sell over 100 books in one day.

But there are a lot of other book promotion sites you could try:

- The Fussy Librarian
  (http://www.thefussylibrarian.com/)
- James Mayfield
  (http://www.jameshmayfield.com/book-promotions/)
- BKnights
  (https://www.fiverr.com/bknights)
- Ebooks Habit
  (http://ebookshabit.com/)

- [Robin Reads](http://robinreads.com/)
  (http://robinreads.com/)
- [Reading Deals](http://readingdeals.com/)
  (http://readingdeals.com/)

Contact your mailing list

Your mailing list is your secret weapon to success as a self-published author. This is your contact book of loyal followers, who, if you take the time to build an authentic and lasting relationship with, are likely to become lifelong customers. I'll get into more detail about this in a bit.

Once you have launched your book, send a shout out to your mailing list with a link to download.

Offer for free through KDP Select

I often see spikes in downloads when doing this and am able to direct more potential
readers to my email list. Increased book downloads can help increase your paid ranking on Amazon, and get you more email subscribers and reviews. It's no secret that good reviews are what sell on Amazon. Use this time to ask your friends to order your book and give an honest review.

After launch

Evaluate your launch campaign

Use Amazon Associates links to check the clicks and conversions. What generated the most sales? How many reviews did you get? What outside platforms brought in the most traffic? Take a look at what's worked, what's fallen short and what you can do better next time. Then, continue building your "author platform" and email list for the next launch.

Guest Blogging

Marketing is an ongoing gig. If you want a steady stream of sales, you really have to spread the word about your book. Guest blogging is a great way of reaching further by getting yourself right in front of your target audience. It's especially valuable if you haven't yet built a solid following of your own.

Guest blogging helps you gain traffic and boost your SEO ranking in a cost-effective way. It helps you establish credibility and authority by providing a valuable article and having your name shown on a reputable site. Once you provide this value, these readers will then go to your site. It also earns you backlinks. Backlinks help your SEO ranking. On top of that, having an article on a highly-ranked site means the post will rank higher on a search engine than it would on your lower-ranking site.

First you need to think about who your intended customers are. Once you know this, you need to determine where they "hang out" online. What do they read? You want to discover out what sites your customers visit and which are relevant to your book. One way of doing this is by including customer development questions in your autoresponders to find this information out.

Now that you know where you want to write, you need to figure out how to get your foot in the door. If it were as simple as just knocking and being let in, then everyone would be guest blogging on the biggest sites.

Having a referral from someone an editor trusts can be a great way to motivate them to publish you. I became a regular contributor to *The Huffington Post* as a result of a long chain of networking events, connections, and follow ups.

But not having the right connections is no excuse for not guest blogging. You can cold email editors—the vast majority of my guest posts have come as a result of cold emails. Get yourself out there as much as possible. It's going to seem scary at first, but you'll get better at it.

Write your next book

There are a million things you could be doing to market your book. You could spend hours on Twitter, send press releases to journalists asking them to write about your book, post on Facebook everyday, and many more…

I've tried most of them. And most of them don't work.

The reality is, most books will fail. After you take the 80/20 approach described in this book, the next best thing you can do is write another book. And with the email subscribers you gained from this book, your next launch will be even more powerful.

You can use it to market your current book, and build your e-mail list even further. Most importantly, the more quality books your write, the more this adds to the professional image of your author page and the more likely potential readers are to buy your books in the future.

Chapter 12

How to Start your First Amazon KDP Ads Campaign

So you've written an awesome book jam-packed with valuable content, had it edited professionally with a beautiful, eye-catching cover designed and uploaded it to Amazon. But getting traffic to your book can be hard in such a crowded market.

Fortunately Amazon is on our side - they recently released their native CPC ads platform - KDP Ads. Now it's not perfect, and myself and some of the authors I've spoken to haven't found it massively profitable, but it can help you sell more books. I think it's especially useful during the launch when getting early downloads can lead to a multiple of additional downloads because Amazon will promote you.

Impressions	Clicks	Average CPC	Detail Page View	Estimated Total Sales ▾
91,275	216	$0.46	267	$41.86
263,503	265	$0.75	338	$26.91
157,485	158	$0.63	201	$17.94
37,999	85	$0.62	94	$15.94
132,771	140	$0.59	175	$11.88

I believe it will grow to become more favorable to authors overtime. As with anything, it's best to get in there and try it out for yourself.

This chapter provides a step-by-step tutorial on how to start your first Amazon KDP ads campaign. I've included advice and best practices based on my most successful campaigns to help you out.

Step 1: Start your first KDP ads campaign in KDP dashboard

Log in to your account at kdp.amazon.com. From your bookshelf select the book you want to promote. Then click "promote and advertise" under the KDP Select column.

Step 2: Click "create an ad campaign"

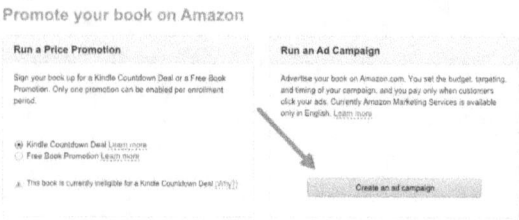

Step 3: Choose your campaign type

Select to either target your ads by keywords (Sponsored Products) or target your ad by product or interest (Product Display Ads). We will run through the steps of Product Display Ads in this post, the process for sponsored products is very similar.

Step 4: Target your ad by products

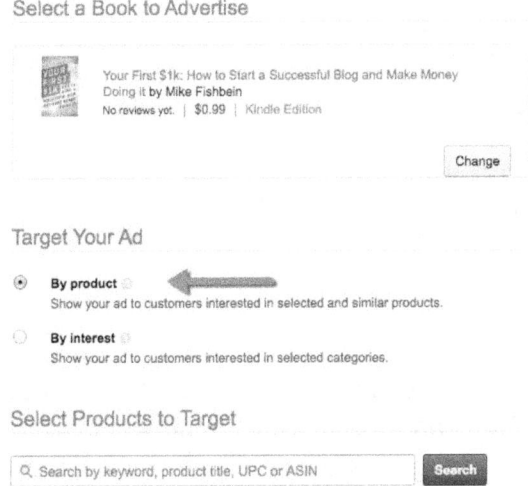

Select a Book to Advertise

Your First $1k: How to Start a Successful Blog and Make Money
Doing it by Mike Fishbein
No reviews yet. | $0.99 | Kindle Edition

Change

Target Your Ad

⦿ **By product**
Show your ad to customers interested in selected and similar products.

○ **By interest**
Show your ad to customers interested in selected categories.

Select Products to Target

🔍 Search by keyword, product title, UPC or ASIN   Search

Targeting your ads by interest means your ads reach
customers based on their browsing history. Targeting
your ads by product shows your ads in the detail
pages of products you handpick yourself. These can
be books, movies or other related products. Try a
selection of books closely related to yours. Run a
couple of different ad campaigns to see which yield
the best results.

Step 5: Select books to target by keyword

Search relevant keywords to find what other books to target. You can either select competing books or books your target readers are likely to be checking out. It pays off to do some research into your target audience's habits and interests so you can make better predictions.

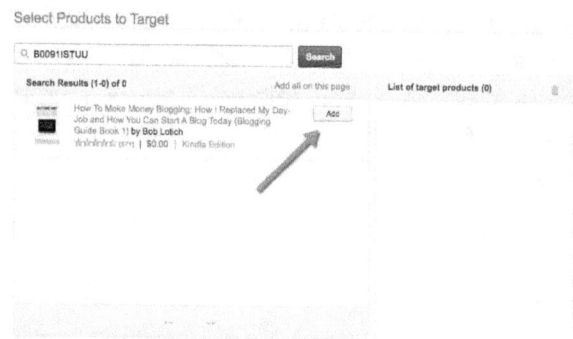

You can search for competing books to target by either typing in keywords or the specific ASIN. Click "add" once you find them.

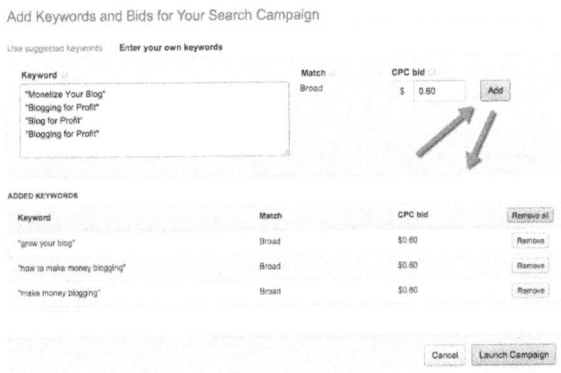

Add Keywords and Bids for Your Search Campaign

For sponsored products, you appear in search results. So, if you're trying to rank on Amazon for a search term like "Self-Publish a Book on Amazon," you could choose this type of campaign to make your book rank higher. Type in the keywords you want to target for.

Step 6: Add a lot of books to increase your impressions

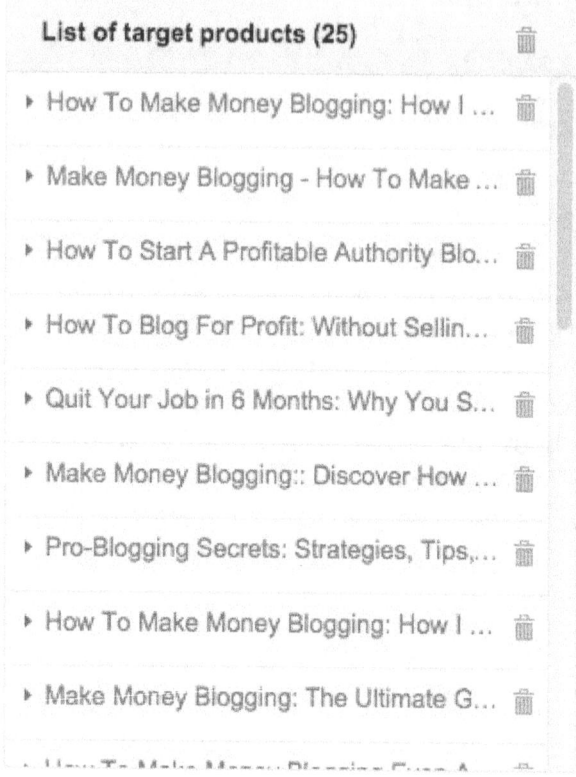

I suggest targeting a large amount this increases the amount of places your ad can be shown and so also increases impressions. Remember, you only pay when your ad is clicked on, not when it is just viewed. Saying this though, if your ad has less than 0.1% CTR (click through rate), Amazon may deem it low relevance and discontinue it. So do your research into who to target.

Step 7: Unselect extend reach

○ Automatically extend your reach to include related products, such as those frequently bought with your book (recommended).

⚠ Because you deselected the option to target related products, your potential number of impressions is greatly reduced.

If you've targeting a lot of relevant books, you probably don't need Amazon to show your book on other books that may not be relevant.

Step 8: Enter in your campaign name, high bid max and budget

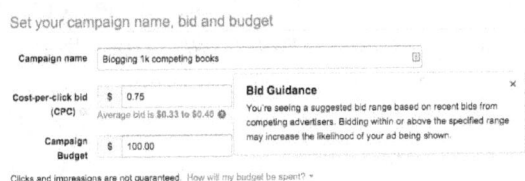

Your cost-per-click-bid is the maximum amount you are willing to pay whenever a potential customer clicks on your ad. The bid guidance Amazon provides is based on the current book price and click to purchase rate. Popular targets have more competition and so higher bid rates. Test targets which are appropriate for you.

The minimum amount for your campaign budget is $100. If you set it for say, $300, you won't necessarlly be charged this full amount, only if you have enough clicks adding up to $300. You're charged 1c more than the next highest bid each time your ad is clicked on.

Step 9: Enter your campaign duration and pacing

Campaign Settings

Start date: 10/08/2015   End date: 11/07/2015

Pacing: ⭕ Deliver my campaign as quickly as possible
🔘 Allow Amazon to spread out my campaign smoothly

Choose how long your campaign will run for and whether you want your budget used up as quickly as possible or spread evenly throughout the duration of your campaign. Your campaign will end either when the end date is reached or your budget dries up, whichever is first. Hover over the question marks to get more information.

Step 10: Enter headline, preview your ad and submit

Create your ad

Headline

How to Make Money Blogging

Characters remaining: 24

Preview your ad

270 x 150   300 x 250   217 x 128   245 x 135   980 x 55

Where will my ad appear? ▾

"How to Make Money Blogging"

Your First $1k: How to Start a Successful Blog ...
Mike Fishbein
$0.99

Cancel   Submit campaign for review

For your headline, don't necessarily just enter in the name of your book. Make sure it draws readers to click on your ad. A preview of your ad is automatically generated using your book's information. Select your dimensions and check the details of your campaign summary.

CAMPAIGN SUMMARY

 Your First $1k: How to Start a Successful Blog and Make Money Doing it
by Mike Fishbein

Locations

Detail pages on Amazon.com

Targeting

Product targeting
25 targeted products added

Campaign settings

Name: **Blogging 1k competing books**
CPC bid: **$0.75**
Budget: **$150.00**

Pacing: **Allow Amazon to spread out my campaign smoothly**
Duration: **10/08/2015 - 11/07/2015**

Double check all the details of your campaign summary, and once your are happy, send it to Amazon for review.

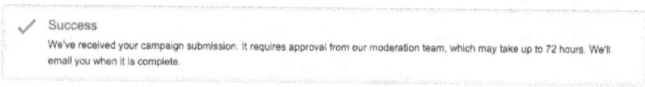

Step 11: Wait for ad approval

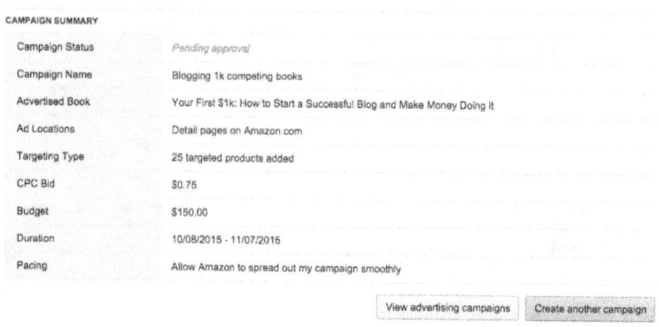

Amazon will approve your ad within the next 72 hours.

You will receive an e-mail when the review is complete. Once it has been approved, you are ready to launch!

Final step 12: Review your stats

Impressions	Clicks	Average CPC	Detail Page View	Estimated Total Sales ▾
91,275	216	$0.46	267	$41.86
263,503	265	$0.75	338	$26.91
157,485	158	$0.63	201	$17.94
37,999	85	$0.62	94	$15.94
132,771	140	$0.59	175	$11.88
64,282	60	$0.74	83	$8.97
94,181	91	$0.63	112	$7.92
15,353	21	$0.10	29	$3.98
8,784	19	$0.49	24	$2.99
3,444	5	$0.44	8	$0.99

You likely won't get your targeting spot on first time round so monitor your status regularly throughout the duration of your campaign. Adjust your bidding and try different targeting strategies.

Status	Campaign Name	Type	Start Date ▾	End Date	Budget	Spend	Impressions	Clicks	Average CPC	Detail Page View	Estimated Total Sales
Pending review	Blogging 1k completing books	Product Display	10/08/2015	11/07/2015	Campaign: $150	$0.00	-	-	-	-	-

As your ad is part of a real time auction, there's no way of seeing how it is doing live, but you can check its status from your advertising campaign screen. I recommend you do this regularly.

Here's a breakdown of the metrics:

- impressions - the number of times your ad has appeared on amazon.com
- clicks - the number of times viewers have clicked on your ad
- average CPC - the average price you pay each time your ad is clicked
- detail page views - the number of times someone who has clicked on your ad has also veiwed your book page

Key Takeaways

KDP ads may not be for everyone but I definitely see merit in it and can see it growing in popularity and effectiveness within the near future.

I think ads can be especially valuable during the first week of your launch, where it's critically important to get a lot of downloads in a short amount of time.

Remember, you can edit, pause or cancel campaigns at any time, so don't be afraid of testing out different methods. See what works, what doesn't work, and adjust your campaign accordingly.

Conclusion

Key Takeaways, Getting Started, and Additional Resources

If you've read this far, you've learned all my best advice for self-publishing a bestseller. Many of these lessons have been learned the hard way: by doing the opposite of almost everything in this book and selling little or no books.

I hope you will use this guide to self-publish your first bestseller, and experience all the rewards that comes with hit.

Despite the amazing opportunities that self-publishing on Amazon presents, many people still make excuses and have fears about doing it. Before I recap some of the most essential strategies discussed in this book, and give you access to my free checklist, I want to squash some of the mindsets that may be holding you back from getting started.

Overcoming Obstacles and Self-Limiting Beliefs

Below are a list of the most common fears and objections I hear people expressing about self-publishing and what I've experienced myself. First I will state the fear, and then I will provide my tips and advice for overcoming it.

Fear of Failure: "What if no one buys my book?"

What if no one likes it? What if the book fails? What if all the time I put into my book is wasted? What will I tell my friends, family, and colleagues?

My advice for overcoming fear of failure:

There's always a risk of failure, but you can't succeed if you don't try. Accept that failure is a possibility, but don't let it cripple you. If it was a guaranteed easy success, everyone would do it.

Your ability to tolerate failure will enable you to seize opportunities that others scare away from.

Imposter's Syndrome: "I'm not an 'expert.'"

Many people think they need to be an "expert" in order to write a book on the topic. They think that they need to have years of experience and be one of the world's best in the field. That may have been true during the old publishing era, but it's certainly not true now.

My advice for overcoming expertise insecurity:

Part of the beauty of self-publishing is that you don't need to be an expert at all. Anyone can do it! Self-publishing has lowered barriers. To get a publishing deal you have to be an "expert," but anyone can, has, and will self-publish. Self-publishing is the new blogging.

First, as a "non-expert," you can relate better to your audience. You may have more relation to the challenges your audience is likely to be experiencing, the questions they may have, and/or the way they might be thinking about them.

There must be some small component of the topic that you're the best at. Secondly, expert is a relative term. I wrote a book on conducting customer development interviews, rather than about Lean Startup as a whole.

The Time To Start: NOW

At some point you have to put down the books, podcast, and blog posts, and start doing.

It feels productive to learn. And there is so much information out there, you could do it all day everyday for the rest of your life.

I've been there all too many times. I go to Quora and end up coming out of some rabbit hole three hours later forgetting why I was there in the first place.

Learning is important and valuable. But time spent consuming is time that could be spent building instead.

Key Takeaways

Starting is the hardest part of self-publishing your own book. But once you do, it's all downhill from there. Below are six critical takeaways to follow to take you from draft to bestseller.

1. Write a book that readers will love

Not all ideas are worth their weight in gold. Do some research into your niche's demands, look up your competitors, and determine just how much money your proposed book could make. There are some great tools for this such as KbookPromotions (http://jvz5.com/c/436931/167361) and K-Lytics.

2. Craft an attention grabbing title and cover

Your title and your cover design are two of the most important elements that will trigger potential readers to your book once they find it via the various marketing strategies discussed in this book. It's well worth it to invest in a professional designer. Throw a line out to your network and see who can help out, this has worked really well for me in the past. Otherwise you can try Upwork or 99designs.

3. Write an attractive sales description for Amazon

This is your chance to really sell your book. Focus on what value readers will get from reading it. Identify their problem and then tell them exactly how your book will solve it.

4. Publish your book on KDP, Createspace and ACX

Having your book in Kindle, paperback, and audiobook will improve the professional image of your book page, enable you to reach new audiences, and can help you make additional streams of income.

5. Plan your book marketing

Having great content and a great cover and title is not enough. It's vital to have you book marketing plan pinned down before launch. There are a number of sites that promote self-published books that you can submit your book to to get huge results. In addition, guest blogging, sending it to your email list, and getting reviews so that Amazon will promote you can be very effective.

6. Write your next book

You've published and launched your book, congratulations! Give yourself a reward and then then get straight back to work creating your next book. Not all books are a success, so it's best to give yourself many chances to succeed. You can use this next book to market your current book and, the more books you write, the more opportunity you have to build your e-mail list. The bigger your e-mail list, the more powerful your book launches get and the more successful you become as a self-published author.

Your Free Checklist

I really want you to succeed. So, I'm going to give you my Ultimate Amazon Self-Publishing Checklist for free. In this comprehensive checklist I'll walk you through each and every step you need to take to self-publish a successful book. From coming up with a book idea right through to the best marketing practices post launch, it's all in there for you.

It's tough to self-publish a book that people want to buy (or even know it exists) let alone it be a great success and get onto Amazon's bestseller list! Believe me I know how difficult it can be. But it is possible! I've done it and now I want to help you do the same.

To guide you through the entire process from coming up with a book idea to landing yourself on the bestseller list, I have created this comprehensive 29 step checklist to guide you all the way through.

Everything I have learnt has been condensed into this one, practical, step-by-step checklist that you can print out and reference as you go along.

>> Get the checklist for free here <<
(http://mfishbein.com/selfpub-checklist-book)